The Difference Christ Makes

The Difference Christ Makes

Celebrating the
Life, Work, and Friendship
of Stanley Hauerwas

EDITED BY

Charles M. Collier

FOREWORD BY

Richard B. Hays

CASCADE *Books* · Eugene, Oregon

THE DIFFERENCE CHRIST MAKES
Celebrating the Life, Work, and Friendship of Stanley Hauerwas

Copyright © 2015 Wipf and Stock Publishers. All rights reserved. Except for brief quotations in critical publications or reviews, no part of this book may be reproduced in any manner without prior written permission from the publisher. Write: Permissions, Wipf and Stock Publishers, 199 W. 8th Ave., Suite 3, Eugene, OR 97401.

Cascade Books
An Imprint of Wipf and Stock Publishers
199 W. 8th Ave., Suite 3
Eugene, OR 97401

www.wipfandstock.com

ISBN 13: 978-1-62564-056-7

Cataloging-in-Publication data:

The difference Christ makes : celebrating the life, work, and friendship of Stanley Hauerwas / edited by Charles M. Collier ; foreword by Richard B. Hays.

x + 104 pp. ; cm.

ISBN 13: 978-1-62564-056-7

1. Hauerwas, Stanley, 1940–. I. Collier, Charles M., 1971–. II. Hays, Richard B. III. Title.

BX4827.H34 D54 2015

Manufactured in the U.S.A.

Contents

Contributors

Charles M. Collier is an Editor at Wipf and Stock Publishers, Eugene, Oregon.

Peter Dula is Associate Professor of Religion and Culture at Eastern Mennonite University, Harrisonburg, Virginia.

Richard B. Hays is Dean and the George Washington Ivey Professor of New Testament at Duke Divinity School, Durham, North Carolina.

Stanley Hauerwas is Gilbert T. Rowe Professor Emeritus of Divinity and Law at Duke University, Durham, North Carolina.

Jennifer A. Herdt is Gilbert L. Stark Professor of Christian Ethics and Religious Studies at Yale University, New Haven, Connecticut.

Charles R. Pinches is Professor and Chair of the Theology and Religious Studies Department at the University of Scranton, Pennsylvania.

Jonathan Tran is Associate Professor of Religion at Baylor University, Waco, Texas.

Samuel Wells is Vicar of St Martin-in-the-Fields, Trafalgar Square, and Visiting Professor of Christian Ethics at King's College, London.

Foreword

THE PAPERS AND RESPONSES in this volume were delivered, fittingly, on All Saints Day, 2013, as part of a day-long event to celebrate the career of Stanley Hauerwas, upon the occasion of his retirement from the faculty of Duke Divinity School. Scores of Stanley's friends and former students came to Durham from all over the U.S. and even from across the seas to honor him and to recognize his extraordinary contributions to the fields of theology and ethics, and to the church. They packed Goodson Chapel all day to listen to a series of insightful lectures that sought to sum up and assess the impact of Stanley's work, and in the evening they packed the ballroom at the Durham Hilton for a celebratory dinner.

There was a lot of laughter that day as stories were recounted about Stanley's iconoclastic irreverence for the tepid conventions of academic discourse. And there were perhaps a few tears shed as friends and colleagues gratefully recalled his generosity of spirit and lamented the closing of a chapter in his academic career.

But the central message of the day was encapsulated in the theme of the whole event: "The Difference Christ Makes." As the different speakers talked about Stanley's paradigm-changing impact on scholarship, one insight came ever more clearly into focus: the deepest theme of Stanley's work, the consistent thread running through all his thought, is his emphasis on the centrality of Jesus Christ. At the end of the day, his work is not defined by the ethics of character, or by pacifism, or by countercultural communitarian ecclesiology. All these elements play important roles in his writings, but they are reflexes or consequences of his more fundamental commitment to think rigorously about the implications of confessing Jesus Christ as Lord. Without Christ at the center, his intellectual project would make no sense. But with Christ as the center, the pieces fall into place:

Stanley's writings stand as a rigorous, surprising, and faithful witness in a world that otherwise lives in confusion and self-deception.

Readers of the present volume can see how this theme unfolds in various ways through the elegant essays offered by Sam Wells, Jennifer Herdt, and Jonathan Tran, along with thought-provoking responses by Charlie Pinches, Peter Dula, and Stanley himself. It is also no accident that the volume is framed by the text of the service of Holy Eucharist for the Feast of All Saints that opened the day and by the homily that Stanley preached on that occasion. Stanley's theology belongs in the context of a worshiping community, a community seeking to live out truthful obedience to God. And it was fitting the celebrant for that Eucharistic service was Stanley's wife Paula Gilbert, his closest friend and companion on his journey.

Special recognition should be given to Zac Koons and Carole Baker for their diligent work in organizing this day of tribute to Stanley, and for making sure it all ran smoothly. Charlie Collier of Wipf and Stock also deserves great credit for gathering and editing the essays in this volume and shepherding it to press.

It has been my deep privilege to count Stanley as a friend and colleague for the past quarter century. I have learned much from him, talked baseball with him, worked together with him on faculty business, and walked a few steps with him along the path of following Jesus. Though he has retired from full-time faculty status, he remains a Senior Research Fellow in the Divinity School, and he is still at work on his writing, still thinking through the difference Christ makes and helping the rest of us think through that difference more faithfully. For that, we are grateful, and we are grateful for the authors of the essays in this volume, who have listened carefully to Stanley's voice and sought to amplify and interpret it. By reading this book, you will join with all of us who were there on All Saints Day, 2013. We invite you to join with us in listening, arguing, laughing, and paying honor to one of God's angular and brilliant saints.

Richard B. Hays
Duke Divinity School
Epiphany, 2015

A Homily on All Saints

Duke Divinity School

November 1, 2013

Stanley Hauerwas

DANIEL 7:1–3, 15–18
PSALM 149
LUKE 6:20–31

WE KNOW MANY OF their names—Mary, Joseph, Paul, Peter, Andrew, Matthew, Stephen, James, Elizabeth, Jude, Augustine, Jerome, Julian, Catherine, Teresa. The list is long, but even if we named all whose names we know, the list of those we do not know is even longer. Most of the saints we celebrate today had names that are now lost to us. The saints of times past and even the present are most often people who lack the power to insure they will be remembered. They are the blessed ones Jesus describes as the poor, the hungry, the mournful.

Many, perhaps most, were ordinary people without formal learning. Their understanding of the Gospel may well have been rudimentary, but they nonetheless were willing to live and even die rather than betray what God had done for them in Christ. The church's celebration of "all saints" is not a lazy attempt to make sure we have them all covered. Rather we celebrate all of the saints, whether remembered by name or not, because without them we would not be. Today is a celebration of the holy communion.

In the Book of Common Prayer we are invited often to thank God for a particular saint. But we are also directed to pray this prayer: "Almighty God, you have knit together your elect in one communion and fellowship in the mystical body of your Son Christ our Lord: Give us grace so to follow your blessed saints in all virtuous and godly living, that we may come to those ineffable joys that you have prepared for those who truly love you; through Jesus Christ our Lord, who with you and the Holy Spirit lives and reigns, on God, in glory everlasting. Amen." This prayer makes no attempt to single out a particular saint but rather thanks God for the gift of those known and unknown who by their fellowship of love and prayer sustain our attempt to be a fellowship of love and prayer.

I confess I find our recognition of these nameless saints to be quite challenging. I am not sure what to make of saints with no name. We live in a world in which few know or want to know our names. Lost in the multitude, we have a desperate hunger to be acknowledged. The hunger to be known, moreover, is compelled by the knowledge of our fleeting existence. Our lives seem quickly to blaze into existence, but the flame is too soon extinguished. The frightening reality is that no matter how famous one might become, we are fated to be forgotten by this world. The act of recognizing the nameless saints, then, forces me to recognize my own desire to be remembered. Why else do I do good if not to be recognized to be a good person? Would I seek to be good if no one were watching?

Yet what seems to make a saint a saint is their refusal to try and insure that they will be remembered. They do not seek to be known by their contemporaries or us, rather they lead lives that exhibit a singular desire to be remembered by God. This is why sainthood is never the aim of the saint; the only pursuit that leads to sainthood is the pursuit of holiness. For as David McCarthy taught me, the saints do not know they are saints until God tells them who they are. It is before the throne of God that the saints learn their true name.

It strikes me as important on this day in which I am to be celebrated that we attend in particular to those saints whose names we do not know. I am under no illusion that I am to be counted among such saints. Yet by having my attention directed toward their lives I learned what my primary task as a theologian was meant to be—that is, to help us draw near to the saints who have drawn near to God.

Our passage from Daniel reminds us that setting apart a day for remembering the "holy ones" is itself a political exercise. The kingdom which the holy ones receive, and which we may hope to receive with them, is set apart from the kingdoms of the earth. Moreover, this kingdom is said to be theirs "forever—forever and ever." It is this same kingdom Christ describes when he distinguishes the blessed from the rich, from those who do not hunger, from those whose possessions make them less than serious, and from those whose worldly recognition becomes their self-satisfaction.

The blessed ones will inherit the kingdom of God because they have learned to live as citizens in the kingdom wrought by Christ; that kingdom is theirs even while still becoming their inheritance. By contrast, those who live according to the politics of the world—that is, those whose ambition is aimed at insuring they will not be forgotten—consequently resist the gift of communion with God's saints and the God who calls them friends.

To celebrate all of the saints, therefore, is to celebrate the reign of the kingdom of God. By remembering all of those who have come before us, we may find comfort in knowing that our citizenship in that kingdom has little to do with whether or not our names, our faces, our good works—all of those things which make us us—will be remembered by those who come after us. Instead our citizenship in that kingdom Christ has brought means we desire first and foremost to be remembered by the One who always goes before us.

So let us rejoice in this day. Let us give thanks for those saints we know by name and yet even more let us give thanks for those saints whose names we do not know, for with them we find a sweet fellowship that only Christ's love can make possible. By being a people who remember the saints—all of the saints—we learn how wonderful it is that we too are remembered by the Lord and made citizens of his heavenly kingdom even now. What a glorious thing to be a people charged with such a memory. So let us remember God's saints on this day and thank God every day for their lives.

1

The Difference Christ Makes

Samuel Wells

Introduction

WE'VE COME TOGETHER TO recognize, not the difference Stanley Hauerwas has made, but the difference Christ makes.

Many of us have become accustomed to hearing Stanley say, "I did not intend to be Stanley Hauerwas."[1] Such an apparently counterintuitive but utterly characteristic observation invites us to a more significant wondering. I wonder whether Jesus Christ truly wanted to be Jesus Christ. If you attend, as George Lindbeck did, to the crusader shouting "Christ is Lord" as he plunges his ax into the head of the Saracen; or if you ponder for very long the way colonialism was concocted out of the trinity of Christianity, commerce, and civilization; or even if you meander through the myriad stalls of Lourdes in the Hautes-Pyrénées with their kitsch renderings of Mary and her son, you would have to say, surely not.[2] Surely Jesus never wanted to be Jesus Christ.

But when Stanley retires: when all the books are finished, all the symposia enjoyed, all the invited lectures given, all the doctoral theses submitted, all the blurbs filed, all the interviews yielded, and all the paraphernalia

---

1. Stanley Hauerwas, *Hannah's Child: A Theologian's Memoir* (Grand Rapids: Eerdmans, 2010) ix.

2. George Lindbeck, *The Nature of Doctrine: Religion and Theology in a Postliberal Age* (Philadelphia: Westminster John Knox, 1984) 64.

of the Stanley Hauerwas that Stanley never intended to become is set aside, what is the difference that Stanley has made? Surely it comes down to this: he has laid bare the difference Christ makes. It is, surely, all that any theologian could aspire to do.

And what is that difference? That is the theme of the day and the subject of my lecture. I begin, as Stanley often does, on a critical note.

The Christ that Makes No Difference

When Bill Clinton came to Duke Chapel in 2009 and spoke at the memorial service for John Hope Franklin, he began with the unforgettable words, "John Hope was an angry, happy man; and a happy, angry man."[3] He could have been talking about Stanley Hauerwas. In the early nineties I wrote a dissertation about Stanley's work; but when I came to turn it into a book I realized I needed to insert a new opening chapter.[4] I called the chapter "From Fate to Destiny" because it fitted with the title of the book, but in reality the chapter was called "Why Stanley Hauerwas is so Angry"—or, to use more of a Stanley word, "Mad." And the reason was, and still is, more or less the same reason Jesus was so angry when he entered the temple on Palm Sunday.[5] And that reason is, in simple language, "I thought this was supposed to be about God." Stanley Hauerwas is mad with the church, and with a significant strand in the theological academy; and what he's mad about is the Christ who makes no difference.

Stanley and I once accepted an invitation to speak together to the annual meeting of the National Association of College and University Chaplains. Speaking with Stanley is a tremendous privilege but also incurs a significant risk. I offered what to the best of my ability was a nuanced and thoughtful but suitably challenging exploration of a Christian view of other faiths.[6] Stanley followed and began with the words, "What you guys probably don't understand is that Sam's just told you you're all dinosaurs.

3. A report of the speech can be found at http://www.dukechronicle.com/articles/2009/06/18/clinton-recalls-angry-happy-man.

4. Samuel Wells, *Transforming Fate into Destiny: The Theological Ethics of Stanley Hauerwas* (Carlisle: Paternoster, 1998; reissued Eugene, OR: Cascade, 2004).

5. Mark 11:15–17 and parallels.

6. The lecture is available as follows: Samuel Wells, "A Christian Vision for Faith Among Other Faiths," *Journal of Inter-Religious Dialogue* 4 (July 18th, 2010) 46–56. Online: http://irdialogue.org/wp-content/uploads/2010/07/Wells-Issue-4-Part-I.pdf.

Sam's an asshole. You may not be aware that for a Texan male that's about as intimate a term of endearment as we have available. But you're not assholes; you're dinosaurs." I saw my future partnership with this distinguished organization going up in smoke in a matter of seconds. I could see that Stanley was, to use his word, and a word not found in older and more reliable manuscripts of the New Testament, "pissed." He was "pissed" (which, to clarify, means in Texan not drunk, but angry) because he took this body of people to epitomize what he believes is wrong with the American church—a church for whom Christ makes no difference.

To understand that judgment we need to comprehend two stories. The first is the story of Christian ethics in America—a book he says he has never written, but one that if we were to tease him, we might say he's written about 30 times.[7] The story goes through four generations, beginning with Walter Rauschenbusch, so much influenced by Albrecht Ritschl, moving to Reinhold and H. Richard Niebuhr, so much shaped by Ernst Troeltsch, and on to James Gustafson and Paul Ramsey, who played such significant roles in Stanley's own development, and then finally to Stanley's contemporaries, who have each, grudgingly or gladly, sooner or later, had to explain how their own judgments converged with or diverged from his.[8]

Perhaps the ghost in this story is Albert Schweitzer. Schweizer's *Quest for the Historical Jesus*, translated into English in 1910, and portraying Jesus as offering a radical ethic suitable for an interim prior to a highly proximate eschaton, seemed to legitimate the dismantling of the Christ who might make any difference.[9] Reinhold Niebuhr's ethic, based on an analysis of human nature, and in Stanley's view methodologically atheist, can't be understood outside the reception history of Schweizer's influential study. But it's for Reinhold Niebuhr that Stanley reserves the sharpest lashings of his whip of cords. "For Niebuhr, God is nothing more than the name of our need to believe that life has an ultimate unity that transcends the world's chaos and makes possible what order we can achieve in this life."[10] Christian doctrine morphs into anthropology, in a way that would make Feuerbach chuckle in his grave. "Justification by faith is loosed from its Christological context

---

7. See "Christian Ethics in America (and the *Journal of Religious Ethics*): A Report on a Book I Will Not Write," in *A Better Hope: Resources for a Church Confronting Capitalism, Democracy, and Postmodernity* (Grand Rapids: Brazos, 2000) 55–69.

8. For more on this story, see Wells, *Transforming Fate into Destiny*, 3–10.

9. Albert Schweitzer, *The Quest of the Historical Jesus* (Mineola, NY: Dover 2005).

10. Stanley Hauerwas, *With the Grain of the Universe: The Church's Witness and Natural Theology* (Grand Rapids: Brazos, 2001) 131.

and made a truth to underwrite a generalized version of humility in order to make Christians trusted players in the liberal game of tolerance."[11] Of course, this was popular and influential: Niebuhr became "the theologian of a domesticated god capable of doing no more than providing comfort to the anxious conscience of the bourgeoisie."[12] Thus theology became ethics, and ethics became about sustaining liberal social orders in a Stoic fashion. This is why Stanley is, as he puts it, so "pissed."

With theologians like Reinhold Niebuhr and Paul Tillich, Stanley believes, who needs secularists and atheists? As Alasdair MacIntyre succinctly puts it, "the church has given the world less and less in which to disbelieve." While the unprovoked verbal assault on the national chaplains' conference was not a little unfair, it's not hard to see how Stanley has come to see chaplaincy as an aspect of the church's ministry that retains the right to be present in rites of passage and suffering and decision-making on the condition that it takes for granted that Christ makes no difference.

Alongside this story of the theological academy comes a parallel story of the church in America. This story has of course many strands, so I am going to isolate but three, which I'm going to call Good Friday, Ascension, and Pentecost.

To start with Good Friday, a very significant part of American Protestantism has placed heavy emphasis on the peril of the human condition in the face of death in general and hell in particular, and has accordingly seen the difference made by Jesus as almost entirely focused on his substitutionary atonement on the cross. This abstraction of the gospel, which renders the evangelists' accounts of Jesus' life and ministry, let alone the entire Old Testament, largely ancillary, clearly assumes Jesus makes an eternal difference, but has little or no place for a temporal one.[13] Even when evangelical impulses broaden the notion of salvation from deliverance from heavenly judgment to earthly well being, the notion that Jesus' life and ministry offer any kind of a template for discipleship remains elusive. It's important to note the correspondence between the conversionist gospel, so significant to the Methodism in which Stanley was raised, with its denial of narrative and discomfort towards moral formation, and decisionist ethics, with its obliviousness to story and character. The seeds of the turn against decisionist

11. Ibid., 136.

12. Ibid., 138.

13. Samuel Wells, *Speaking the Truth: Preaching in a Pluralistic Culture* (Nashville: Abingdon, 2008) 155–61.

ethics that so significantly marked Stanley's early academic career were planted in the gospel halls of his youth.[14]

Moving to Ascension, Jesus becomes invisible. As Scott Bader-Saye explains, this is because all God's promises to Israel are being fulfilled—only not in Jesus. There is a messiah, but that Messiah is America. America has become Jesus. It has not just become the new Israel, it has become Jesus. In the gospels it is hard to speak of Church in the presence of Jesus, and thus Pentecost seems a fitting beginning for the church. In just the same way it is hard to speak of Church in America, because America is Jesus. America has become the embodiment of the way God overcomes evil and brings life.[15] As Stanley puts it, "The subject of Christian ethics in America has always been America."[16]

And turning to Pentecost, there is a close link between American democracy and some of the assumptions of many Protestant believers. The Holy Spirit has come upon God's people: thus everyone can meet God for themselves, uninhibited by background or identity; thus also God acts deeply in people's lives, so much that it may seem that this is God's *raison d'être*, and that all other actions of God may be accorded status with reference to God's definitive revelation to them; and thus that the day of the Lord is no longer the day of cross or of resurrection, but the day I was reborn. Hence God becomes a character in a story that is fundamentally about me.[17]

Stanley knows his church. He points out that once, Catholics believed in the transformation at the altar and the power of absolution, so they forgave flaws in their priest's character. Meanwhile Protestants believed in the power of preaching and could thus forgive weakness in clerical handling of finance. But now we've lost belief in such sacerdotal power so we want the minister to keep moral rules we can't live up to ourselves and have a model family.[18] In a footnote (where the seasoned reader of Stanley's work expects to find the true gold), Stanley summarizes what makes him so angry:

14. Samuel Wells, "Stanley Hauerwas," in Ian Markham, ed., *The Blackwell Companion to the Theologians, Volume Two: Enlightenment to the Twenty-First Century* (Malden, MA: Wiley-Blackwell, 2009) 277–93.

15. Wells, *Speaking the Truth*, 12–16. See Scott Bader-Saye, *Church and Israel After Christendom: The Politics of Election* (Boulder: Westview) 65–66.

16. Hauerwas, "On Being a Christian and an American," in *A Better Hope*, 23–34.

17. Wells, *Speaking the Truth*, 8–12.

18. Stanley Hauerwas, "Clerical Character," in *Christian Existence Today: Essays on Church, World, and Living in Between* (Durham, NC: Labyrinth 1987) 133.

> The greatest immorality of the contemporary ministry is its will-
> ingness to substitute socialization for belief in God. . . . Pastors
> fail to challenge the congregation to trust that God creates and
> sustains the church. As a result the church becomes a means of
> underwriting the dominant ethos of our culture, the social status
> of members, rather than being a people who think nothing is more
> important than the worship of God.[19]

Those who love reading Stanley Hauerwas are those who read a sentence
like that and hear a cry that meets their place of deep distress and longing.

The Difference Christ Makes

In *Hannah's Child* Stanley can keep silent no longer but finally confesses
that he became a theologian because he couldn't get saved.[20] The irony
is that his theological writing "got Jesus" once his philosophical ethical
credentials were already established. What Jeffrey Stout regards as impossible—that Stanley can encompass Alasdair MacIntyre and John Howard
Yoder—is precisely what makes Stanley's work distinctive.[21] What first
drew me to Stanley's work is that I found in his writing an almost unique
ability to encompass God as God is and the church as the church is—being neither instrumental about the former nor pious about the latter. I
found a disarming humility about the truth-claims of Christianity and a
healthy skepticism about the superiority of any truth-claims to be found
elsewhere—being neither naïve about the former nor over-impressionable
about the latter. I found an eagerness to make plain the practical implications of the Christian faith and a willingness to endure the complexity and
contingency of life in the world—being neither simplistic about the former
nor discouraged by the latter.

Christian doctrine in general, and the creeds in particular, rest on
two fundamental acts of holding-together. The first is the holding-together
of belief in the divinity of Christ with belief in the oneness of God. This
holding-together yields the Trinity. The second is the holding-together of
Christ's full humanity with his full divinity. This holding-together yields the

19. Ibid., 147 n. 21

20. Hauerwas, *Hannah's Child*, 1.

21. Jeffrey Stout, *Democracy and Tradition* (Princeton: Princeton University Press,
2004).

incarnation. Most heresies and arguably most failures of the church come down to the failure to hold together what God has so joined.

And it is this insistence on holding together what most theologians and church people separate that constitutes the distinctiveness of Stanley's depiction of Christ. It becomes clear that being a theologian, for Stanley, means attending to the difference Christ makes. In the spirit of the opening to Stanley's celebrated book *A Community of Character*, I shall therefore now summarize in ten theses what Stanley takes to be the difference Christ makes.[22] I shall concentrate in what follows on three books, *A Community of Character*, *The Peaceable Kingdom*, and *With the Grain of the Universe*, because I take these to be the Christological center of Stanley's work and hence his most abiding achievement. Each thesis that follows rests on Stanley's resistance to making separations that end up by portraying a Christ that makes no difference.

1. *It is not possible to separate Jesus from the narrative of his life.*

Stanley points out that the early Christians began with a story of Jesus. "Their 'Christology' did not consist first in claims about Jesus' ontological status, though such claims were made; their Christology was not limited to assessing the significance of Jesus' death and resurrection, though certainly these were attributed great significance; rather their 'Christology,' if it can be called that, showed the story of Jesus as absolutely essential for depicting the kind of kingdom they now thought possible through his life, death, and resurrection."[23] And this story is intrinsic to what it means to know who Jesus is: "Jesus is he who comes to initiate and make present the kingdom of God through his healing of those possessed by demons, by calling disciples, telling parables, teaching the law, challenging the authorities of his day, and by being crucified at the hands of Roman and Jewish elites and raised from the grave. Insisting that Jesus is the initiator and presence of the kingdom, of course, does not mean he was not the Christ, or that he is not God incarnate, or that his death and resurrection has nothing to do with the forgiveness of sins, but it does mean that each of these claims are subsequent to the whole life of this man whom God has

22. Hauerwas, *A Community of Character: Toward a Constructive Christian Social Ethic* (Notre Dame, IN: University of Notre Dame Press, 1981).

23. Hauerwas, *The Peaceable Kingdom: A Primer in Christian Ethics* (London: SCM, 1984) 73.

claimed as decisive to his own for the presence of his kingdom in this world."[24]

2. *It is not possible to separate Jesus from the early church.*

Stanley is skeptical of skeptics, and suspicious of all who seek to drive a wedge between the so-called Jesus of history and the Christ of faith—and ethics. He is "quite content to assume that the Jesus we have in Scripture is the Jesus of the early church."[25] And this is all to the good, "since the very demands Jesus placed on his followers means he cannot be known abstracted from the disciples' response. The historical fact that we only learn who Jesus is as he is reflected through the eyes of his followers, a fact that has driven many to despair because it seems they cannot know the real Jesus, in fact is a theological necessity. For the 'real Jesus' did not come to leave us unchanged, but rather to transform us to be worthy members of the community of the new age."[26] Here in characteristic fashion Stanley takes what the academy has often found a flaw in the tradition and shows how the church may make it a virtue.

3. *It is not possible to separate Jesus' meaning from his story.*

This claim has more of a bearing on the distinctiveness of Jesus in relation to significant figures in other faith traditions. "There is no moral point or message that is separable from the story of Jesus as we find it in the gospels. There can be no Christ figure because Jesus is the Christ. Jesus' identity is prior to the 'meaning' of the story. There is no meaning that is separable from the story itself. And that is why there can be no easy parallels between the story of Jesus and other redeemer-redemption accounts."[27] Stanley quotes Hans Frei to the effect that "The gospel story's indissoluble connection with an unsubstitutable identity in effect divests the savior story of its mythical quality. The Gospel story is a demythologization of the savior myth because the savior figure is fully identified with Jesus of Nazareth."[28]

24. Ibid., 74.

25. Ibid., 73.

26. Ibid.

27. Hauerwas, *Community of Character*, 42–43.

28. Hans Frei, *The Identity of Jesus Christ*, 59, quoted in Hauerwas, *Community of Character*, 43.

4. *It is not possible to separate Jesus' person from his work.*

Stanley points out the dangers of soteriology determining the shape of Christology. He quotes Wolfhart Pannenberg to suggest that it results in projecting onto Jesus "the human desire for salvation and deification, of human striving after similarity to God, of the human duty to bring satisfaction for sins committed, of the human experience of bondage in failure, in the knowledge of one's own guilt, and most clearly in neo-Protestantism, projections of the idea of perfect religiosity, of perfect morality, of pure personality, of radical trust?"[29] Stanley points out that the opposite desire, to concentrate on the person and not the work, has invariably resulted in imagining a Jesus who was the best version of a moral life—thus for Walter Rauschenbusch Jesus democratized the concept of God and taught the infinite worth of each personality.[30] Jesus' life becomes instrumentalized either way.

5. *It is not possible to separate Jesus from the cross.*

Stanley follows John Howard Yoder in his sense of the significance of the cross. We are called to imitate Jesus not in a general way, copying his external actions one by one, but in a specific way, by appreciating what it meant for him to walk to the cross, thereby renouncing, as Yoder would put it, establishment responsibility and sectarian withdrawal. Being like Jesus means "seeing in his cross the summary of his whole life." It means "to join him in the journey through which we are trained to be a people capable of claiming citizenship in God's kingdom of nonviolent love—a love that would overcome the powers of this world, not through coercion and force, but through the power of this one man's death."[31]

6. *It is not possible to separate Jesus from the kingdom of God.*

Stanley follows Karl Barth in refusing to separate the kingdom from its herald. In Barth's words, "Jesus is himself the established kingdom of God"—what Origen called the *autobasileia*, the kingdom in person. Stanley quotes Julian Hartt, who says that "In the New Testament representation of Jesus Christ his authority and identity are

29. Wolfhart Pannenberg, *Jesus: God and Man* 47, quoted in Hauerwas, *Community of Character*, 42.

30. Hauerwas, *Community of Character*, 42.

31. Hauerwas, *Peaceable Kingdom*, 76.

absolutely inseparable from each other. The Church cannot in good faith try to separate what the Holy Spirit has joined. Jesus Christ is its only valid warrant for preaching the Kingdom of God."[32] This is an especially significant point in relation to social justice movements today. There is always a temptation to assume Jesus was a more or less accurate prophet of the kinds of social relations we see more clearly and practice more truly in our own generation—relations we often call the kingdom. But Stanley insists, with Barth, that we do not have a prior knowledge of what freedom and justice mean, and then see them well expressed in Jesus and consequently call him Lord; quite the contrary, we see Jesus, and he teaches us what freedom and justice and the kingdom entail.

7. *It is not possible to separate knowing Jesus from being his disciple.*

This seventh thesis blows a hole in the historical critical quest and separates Stanley from religion departments across the nation and beyond. Stanley sees that the gospels are written "not only to display Jesus' life, but to train us to situate our lives in relation to that life." Hence "we cannot know who Jesus is and what he stands for without learning to be his followers." The reason for this is that we can project all sorts of needs, dreams, and aspirations onto Jesus. "You cannot know who Jesus is after the resurrection unless you have learned to follow Jesus during his life. His life and crucifixion are necessary to purge us, like his disciples and adversaries had to be purged, of false notions about what kind of kingdom Jesus had brought."[33] Thus Stanley assumes an order of Christian knowing. Metaphysical and anthropological theories must not be allowed "to substitute for the necessary witnessing of Christian lives and communities to the significance of his story." If people fear this means the "real" Jesus will be lost, Stanley retorts that "there is no 'real' Jesus except as he is known through the kind of life he demanded of his disciples . . . . The demand for 'historical accuracy' is ahistorical insofar as the Gospels exhibit why the story of this man is inseparable from how that story teaches us to follow him."[34]

32. Hauerwas, *Community of Character*, 45.
33. Hauerwas, *Peaceable Kingdom*, 74.
34. Hauerwas, *Community of Character*, 44–42.

8. *It is not possible to separate Jesus from social ethics.*

This is perhaps the simplest way to express the difference Stanley has made to Christian ethics in our day. Stanley's work makes this statement a truism. It is probably a truism for almost everyone gathered to hear this lecture today. But it wasn't a truism when Stanley began his career, and there are many places in the theological academy where it remains at best a dubious contention. The point is that Jesus, his person and his work, redefines what is meant by words like political and economic, and even ecological and sexual. Stanley finds Walter Rauschenbush grasping this point in words that could have been written by Yoder: "Truth asks no odds. She will not ask that her antagonist's feet be put in shackles before she will cross swords with him. Christ's Kingdom needs not the spears of Roman legionaries to prop it, not even the clubs of Galilean peasants. Whenever Christianity shows an inclination to use constraint in its own defense or support, it thereby furnishes presumptive evidence that it has become a thing of this world, for it finds the means of this world adapted to its end."[35] I would suggest the theological issue here is the sufficiency of Christ. When social ethics move beyond or outside Jesus, they presuppose that God in Christ had somehow not finished the work of redemption—that it remains incomplete, flawed, partial, insufficient. But Stanley, with Barth, believes that in Christ God gives us more than enough—for ethics, for life, for joy, for glory. If we experience life as insufficient it's because we haven't drawn on the abundance of Christ, not because that abundance isn't there. The desire to articulate an "ethic for everyone," so dear to the hearts of figures from Immanuel Kant to Joseph Fletcher, is a project designed to save the world without the difference Christ makes. This must appear, to a Christian, both doomed and incoherent.

9. *It is not possible to separate the religious from the social.*

One cannot offer a survey of the difference Christ makes as described by Stanley Hauerwas without acknowledging that a major reason why Stanley's ethics "got Jesus" was because Stanley got John Howard Yoder. And so the argument Stanley is walking into is in many ways an argument Yoder is already having with Ernst Troeltsch and

---

35. Walter Rauschenbusch, *The Righteousness of the Kingdom*, 92–93, in Hauerwas, *Community of Character*, 46.

Troeltsch's inheritors, notably H. Richard Niebuhr. For Troeltsch, it is clear that the New Testament is focused on issues that are "always purely religious, dealing with such questions as the salvation of the soul, monotheism, life after death, purity of worship, the right kind of congregational organization" and so on.[36] Troeltsch dismisses any notion that the proclamation of the kingdom had any significant social agenda; instead Jesus aspired to a world in which "all the values of pure spirituality would be recognized and appreciated at their true worth." Yoder's landmark first chapter of his study *The Politics of Jesus* identifies this among various reasons why Jesus is taken to be irrelevant for social ethics. He had an interim ethic, he was a simple agrarian figure, he had no political power, he was largely concerned with self-understanding, he relativized all temporal values, or he came to provide forgiveness not an ethic.[37] But Troeltsch and his inheritors assume that a social ethic has to inform government—he misses the irony that the forms of social organization he highlights as obviously irrelevant offer the promise of a significantly different kind of politics. Jesus challenges the distinction between the religious and the social; in order to preserve it, Troeltsch has to distort Jesus. Much of the church and the theological academy have followed suit.

10. *It is not possible to separate Jesus from Israel.*

Both extremes of Christology—those that concentrate exclusively on Jesus' person and those that concentrate exclusively on Jesus' work—have a problem with the Jews. On the one hand, an overconcentration on the atonement, shorn of narrative and focused on the cross alone, airbrushes Israel out of the economy of salvation. The Old Testament has almost no role, except perhaps, pre-Abraham (and thus pre-Jew), as offering an account of the Fall. On the other hand, Stanley points out that "When Jesus is treated as the perfect example or teacher of morality he turns out to be remarkably anti-Semitic. For then it must be shown that the Jews were somehow morally deficient, if not degenerate, to reject the obvious moral superiority of Jesus."[38] As early as 1981 we find Stanley saying "Central to my position is the assumption

36. Hauerwas, *Community of Character*, 38.

37. John Howard Yoder, *The Politics of Jesus: Behold The Lamb! Our Victorious Lamb* (2nd ed., Grand Rapids: Eerdmans, 1994) 1–20.

38. Hauerwas, *Community of Character*, 235 n. 27.

that Jesus' significance can only be appreciated by recognizing the continued significance of Judaism."[39] Looking to the Old Testament, Stanley maintains that for Israel, seeking God, remembering God's ways and acts, and imitating God were more or less identical. The role of the prophets was to highlight the interconnection of the three. This is how the early Christians came to understand Jesus' life, death, and resurrection. "They had found a continuation of Israel's vocation to imitate God and thus in a decisive way to depict God's kingdom for the world. Jesus' life was seen as a recapitulation of the life of Israel and thus presented the very life of God in the world. By learning to imitate Jesus, to follow in his way, the early Christians believed they were learning to imitate God, who would have them be heirs of the kingdom."[40] Such words more or less summarize Stanley's theology.

I have taken time to set out these ten theses, as much as possible in Stanley's own words, because in so doing I have attempted to identify the epicenter of his theology, and thus to go some way to explaining why we are all here. In what remains of the lecture I want to look at perhaps the two principal lines of criticism of Stanley's theology, each of which I take to be traceable to a reading of the difference Christ makes, before looking at the significance of the difference Stanley proposes.

The Difference Christ's Body Makes

The church, says Stanley, "is the gathering of a people who are able to sustain one another through the inevitable tragedies of our lives. They are able to do so because they have been formed by a narrative, constantly reenacted through the sharing of a meal, that claims nothing less than that [the tragic character of our existence has been taken into God's very life]."[41] The significance of this community is such that Stanley claims, in perhaps his most notorious statement, that "the first social task of the church is to be the church."[42] I want briefly to look at five ways in which this claim rests on the difference Christ makes.

39. Ibid., 236 n. 27.
40. Hauerwas, *Peaceable Kingdom*, 78.
41. Hauerwas, *Community of Character*, 108.
42. Ibid., 109.

Number one, this claim assumes Christ makes a difference—indeed, all the difference. The church does not have to do Christ's work for him. The world has been saved. Its destiny does not hang in the balance, waiting for the church's decisive and timely intervention to tip the scales. The church must not talk or act as if God were dependent on its faithfulness or initiative. The church does not make the difference. The church lives in the difference Christ has made.

Number two, being the church isn't easy! Stanley's phrase—the church's first task is to be the church—is often derided as if the church should be much more ambitious and set its sights on worthier goals. There are no worthier goals. This is partly because forming and sustaining a community of character, challenging and accompanying people as they walk the way of the cross, and holding to the triangle of forgiveness, trust, and discipline is the hardest work there is. With acknowledgement to Aristotle and Peter DeVries, the life of the world may not be worth living but the life of the church is no bowl of cherries either.[43] Stanley often quotes the largest of the countless signs on his office door: "A modest proposal for peace: Let the Christians of the world agree that they will not kill each other."[44] The point is that what sounds modest is currently way beyond our scope, as it has been for most of Christian history.

Not only is being the church not as easy as its cultured patronizers assume, but the existence of the church is foundational for any notion of what constitutes social ethics. What happened to Jesus wasn't an accident. It constitutes the difference Christ makes, and the world's abiding hostility to what Christ is and represents—God's commitment never to be except to be with us. "Even though the world is God's creation and subject to God's redemption it continues eschatologically to be a realm that defies [God's] rule." The church must "provide the institutional space for us to rightly understand the disobedient, sinful, but still God-created character of the world."[45]

Number three, the difference between church and world is simply put: Christ. Making being church prior to the church's other social commitments is a statement of trust rather than fear, and humility rather than

43. Stanley Hauerwas, "The Pathos of the University: The Case of Stanley Fish," in *The State of the University: Academic Knowledges and the Knowledge of God* (Malden, MA and Oxford, UK: Blackwell) 76.

44. Poster image found at http://www.disa.ukzn.ac.za/index.php?option=com_displaydc&recordID=pos00000000.043.053.2231.

45. Hauerwas, *Community of Character*, 92.

arrogance. The church does not have a view on the nature, or even the destiny, of those who do not recognize Christ. It certainly doesn't claim them as Christians (for example, because it respects or admires some quality in them); neither does it take unto itself an assumed responsibility for directing the cultural mainstream (for example, because it sees itself for epistemological or historical reasons as having a privileged angle on the good, the true, and the beautiful); nor does it claim a theory of truth that can knock all other accounts stone dead. None of these assumptions is appropriately derived from commitment to the universality of Christ. Instead, the difference in Christ is that Christ's lordship reaches "beyond the number of those who call him by his right name."[46] Shadrach, Meshach and Abednego know that their God is lord of the whole earth; that doesn't mean they seize power or assume a natural right to rule or endow all people of goodwill as like themselves; but they know that God's ways will win out in the end, even if they don't live to see it. Like Jesus, the church offers a "real option," because of its notion of witness. The church doesn't believe there is "a universal truth which others must also 'implicitly' possess or have sinfully rejected." Hence it believes people only come to the truth by being confronted by the truth.[47]

Number four, and at the risk of oversimplification, the difference Christ makes is this: peace. Stanley broadly accepts Yoder's notion that Christ's way lies between establishment responsibility and sectarian withdrawal, in a witness of radical social nonconformity. This is made possible because Christ's death and resurrection constitute the grain of the universe, and thus the weapons of the world are to be rejected not because they are too strong but because they are too weak. The church has to start by being the church because no other movement or coalition offers theological nonviolence of this kind. Plenty offer pragmatic nonviolence—a set of tactics that can work well provided the adversary has principles to which they may be called back or through which they may be called to account. But only the church has a theological nonviolence that believes this is the way Christ makes the difference, this is the way Christ redeems the world.

Number five, to say the church's first task is to be the church is not to say this is the church's only task. The church's participation in struggles for justice and freedom and dignity and respect and peace are taken for

---

46. John Howard Yoder, "The Basis of Barth's Social Ethics," quoted in Hauerwas, *Community of Character*, 93.

47. Hauerwas, *Community of Character*, 105.

granted, rather than excluded; the point is that if the church is to know what it is doing in such struggles it must be imbued with the difference Christ makes. "As Christians we are committed to the view that justice is possible between peoples because trust is finally a deeper reality in our lives than distrust, because God's justice is more profound than injustice."[48] Yet if being the church were not the prior task of the church, how would Christians remember what the world would never tell them—that forgiveness is the justice of God? That's the difference Christ makes.

The Difference Difference Makes

The word "difference" has come to have a particular resonance in the contemporary theological academy. Over recent generations the realization has grown in church and academy that institutional Christianity in general and theological inquiry in particular have been in the grip of an elite that have shaped them by their own assumptions and to their own purposes, as elites have done in society since time began. The permeability of the elite is disputed but the dominance of those who look like I do and have tended to regard entry as theirs to bestow is more or less beyond question. And that dominance has been expressed in institutional governance, administration, membership, and prominence, in the content of theology, including whose voices and which perspectives are considered normative, and in the process by which theology is communicated and animated and engaged.

And in theological communities that talk about difference more readily than they talk about Christ, and increasingly find it hard to talk about Christ without talking about difference—where, in short, difference has come to name the most tender and disputed areas in the discourse—four questions emerge.

- One is, what do we each, together and separately, do with the anger and the guilt that surface so readily as injustice is recalled and imbalance is highlighted and change seems slow and not everyone seems to allow lives and research trajectories and courses of study to be reshaped accordingly?

- Another is, given that society and university and church and seminary are so embedded in the economics and processes of privilege, is there

48. Hauerwas, *Community of Character*, 110.

a genuine alternative to hand that does not threaten to jettison the partial transformation that has already been made?

- A third is, given that all methods reflect and create elites of different kinds, is there a genuine alternative method that doesn't replicate dominant patterns of power and exclusion.

- And a fourth is, is Christ inextricable from the patterns of domination so many see him as exposing and unraveling—or does Christ truly make a difference, transcending the suspicion and distrust existing so broadly in the academy about almost all forms of knowing and communicating?

This is perhaps the most important question currently facing the academy in which Stanley has made such a difference—a difference he's made by pointing to the difference Christ makes. Stanley has been challenged subtly and less subtly about his reluctance to dispense definitive answers to questions like the ones I've mentioned, or to express sufficient anger towards institutions and methods that seem in the eyes of many to embody an unreconstructed social model. If he has had an impatience towards such questions (and let's acknowledge that impatience constitutes the foothills of anger) it has been that too often they have taken place without the expectation of further discovery of the difference Christ makes.

If one looks at the Syrophoenician woman and her answer to Jesus, "Even the dogs under the table eat the children's crumbs," one realizes three things: one, that, hard as it is for many of his students and readers and audiences to grasp, Stanley has, largely because of reasons of class, spent much of his life feeling much like the woman—excluded, patronized, insulted, and certainly more like her than like Jesus; two, that Christ made the difference in her life, even though it took a lot of elbows and straight talking and overturning of pernicious divisions to get there; and three, that the woman took for granted the difference Christ makes, and that motivated and sustained her through controversy and tension, bringing salvation not just to her but to her daughter, and renewing for the whole church an understanding of the difference Christ makes.[49] She may be our guide in troubled times.

---

49. Mark 7:28.

Making a World of Difference

Stanley has directed around 75 doctoral dissertations—more than any other professor at Duke University. He has probably caused more mischief in the theological imaginations of his students and hearers of his occasional lectures and readers of his books than any other professor the Divinity School has ever had. But he's not under any illusion that such things constitute making a difference. There is only one fundamental difference, and that's the difference Christ makes. The tour de force of his argument in this regard is his Gifford Lectures, *With the Grain of the Universe*, and especially his chapters on Karl Barth. It is Barth who articulates most explicitly the difference Christ makes.

In this case the difference is between two kinds of natural theology. The Gifford style of natural theology yields the question, "How do we know God?" But Barth's question is, "Who is God?" The answer to Barth's question is that God is the one who has chosen never to be except to be with us in Christ. And Barth's answer also answers the Gifford question. But no answer that begins with the Gifford question can answer Barth's question. Natural theology is a sophisticated example of the kind of reasoning that I referred to at the beginning as making Stanley so angry, because it domesticates truth. For Barth, the greater danger is not that humans may misunderstand and reject the gospel, but that they may possess it and render it innocuous.[50] Through the *Church Dogmatics*, Barth seeks to train Christians to be faithful witnesses, disciplining them in their habits of speech and in what he calls "the necessary, thrilling and beautiful tasks which are fruitful for the Church and for the world."[51] Only thus can they gain a theological metaphysics, and see the universe as it truly is.

This is the claim that Stanley should be famous for. He's rightly exasperated answering endless questions about whether he thinks the church should be involved in society and whether he thinks rights are wrong. Because his boldest, most outrageous claim is this: that Jesus is the shape of natural theology. God in Christ, the Christ of cross of resurrection, is the power and the spirit that undergirds the workings of the planets and the stars and the animals and the winds. Jesus is the logic of the universe, and that logic has become flesh and been among us. There is a logic and we can know it because it is shaped to meet us and be with us; and we have beheld

50. Hauerwas, *With the Grain of the Universe*, 198 n. 53.
51. Ibid., 179.

its glory; and despite our utter rejection it has turned death to life and met us beyond our rejection; and we find our peace with ourselves, with one another, and with the creation in sharing this joy. That is the difference Christ makes.

Such difference requires not proof, but witnesses. Witnesses are "people whose practices exhibit their committed assent to a particular way of structuring . . . 'how the world is arranged.'"[52] We're gathered today to salute a happy, angry man, not because he or we are under any illusion that he's made a difference, but because he's been a witness. He has relentlessly displayed the Christological center of the church's witness, a peaceable alternative to the death that grips the world. He has shown how Christians live "with the grain of the universe," and thus he has demonstrated the difference that is made by being Christian. The difference of Stanley Hauerwas is simply this: he has shown the difference Christ makes.

52. Stanley Hauerwas, *With the Grain of the Universe*, 214.

2

Truthfulness and Continual Discomfort

Jennifer A. Herdt

It is a special honor for me to be speaking to you on this occasion. I have never been Stanley Hauerwas's student, nor have I been his faculty colleague, so it is actually something of a mystery to me why I have been invited here today. I know Stanley almost exclusively from conversations at the Society of Christian Ethics over the years. Yet in another sense, I feel that I have been both his student and his colleague, and indeed that he has embraced me in a generous friendship I have done nothing to earn. Apart from being opposites in terms of temperament and personality, we have a lot in common, as it happens: I, too, have Methodist roots but now worship in the Anglican communion; I, too, owe much of my theological sensibilities to my time on the faculty of Theology at Notre Dame; in fact, we left Notre Dame at almost exactly the same age; we both have been formed by time at Yale, though in different eras and at different points in our lives; we both had to learn what it means to teach at a seminary. I can still recall the flash of excitement I felt when I first discovered Stanley's writings—I believe it was *A Community of Character*, though it may have been *The Peaceable Kingdom*. I had left college burdened with a bleak narrative of modernity's inexorable march toward secularization, and was now reading Aquinas, Wittgenstein, Alasdair MacIntyre, and Jeffrey Stout. I had been electrified by *After Virtue*'s diagnosis of the failure of the Enlightenment project of justifying modernity, but it was unclear to me how a retrieval of virtue ethics could be anything but an impotent expression of nostalgia. In the absence of a broadly shared substantive conception of the good life and a tradition in which this had its home, how could the language of the virtues help to address the interminable disagreements of contemporary society? And how could Christian faith be anything but a form of self-deception for those familiar with the story of modernity? In Stanley's writings I found release; I recovered the freedom to own my faith.

I have to admit, though, that reading *The Peaceable Kingdom* did not adequately prepare me for the first time I heard Stanley speak. It was the first meeting of the Society of Christian Ethics that I attended, while a graduate student at Princeton. I walked into the crowded lecture hall with great anticipation. I was not a pacifist, but I had certainly been entranced by the writings of this spokesperson for the nonviolent way of Jesus. I was utterly taken aback by the brash, foul-mouthed Texan who held the stage. I had overlooked the point where he notes that "by disposition I am not much inclined to nonviolence."[1] It took me some time to appreciate that this was not just genuine Stanley, though it was that, but also a deftly placed critique of the class bias that permeates the academy. I was no less astounded when, finding myself (a year or two later) in an elevator with this famous senior professor, he struck up a conversation, took an interest in what I was up to, and never ever afterwards forgot who I was. He has a gift for treating a student like a colleague while at the same time accepting the delicate responsibilities of mentoring. For his excessive generosity, then and ever since, I have been grateful.

Not long ago, I had the opportunity, at Charlie Pinches' invitation, to examine at some length Stanley's transformative contributions to Christian reflection on the virtues. Here I want to do something different: to reflect on where Stanley has brought us in our efforts to think about the church-world relationship. I want to rehearse two simple points this afternoon. First, even if it is indeed the case that the world cannot know itself to be the world without the help of the church, it is also the case that the church cannot help us to speak truthfully unless it speaks not just to, but also with, the world. This is an argument worth making not because Stanley denies it, but because people have not always understood how and why he affirms it. The second is a point well made by James McClendon, and quoted somewhere, I am sure, by Stanley: "The line between the church and the world still

---

1. Stanley Hauerwas, *The Peaceable Kingdom* (Notre Dame: University of Notre Dame Press, 1983) xxiv.

passes through the heart of every believer, and, we may now add, through the heart of every churchly practice as well."[2]

That the church does not *have* a social ethic but rather *is* a social ethic is perhaps Stanley's most famous mantra. This goes hand in hand with his claim that the greatest contribution that the church can make to the world is to be itself, not to go about trying to change the world, but to offer a contrast community by way of which the world may begin to know itself truthfully.[3] This sort of statement, often paired with trenchant critiques of liberalism, has elicited much criticism over the years. But even when Stanley has called for uninvolvement in the world, this has never amounted to a form of *indifference* to the society we inhabit. Take "The Church and Liberal Democracy," published in 1981 in *A Community of Character*. Stanley here insists that "the church and Christians must be uninvolved in the politics of our society and involved in the polity that is the church."[4] But this comment comes within the context of an argument about how Christians can best contribute to the societies in which they find themselves. That argument is that the church must be Christians' primary polity, that the church must assist Christians to develop the skills necessary to live truthfully. By virtue of carrying out the task of forming themselves as a society built on truth rather than fear, Christians are *serving* whatever societies they inhabit, not withdrawing or turning away from them in indifference. In *A Better Hope*, Stanley puts the point differently, confessedly weary of hearing criticism of his advice to Christians to be uninvolved. "I have never sought to justify Christian withdrawal from social and political involvement; I have just wanted us to be involved as Christians."[5] In a very real sense, and despite his criticism of the implicit assumption that the subject of Christian ethics in America is America, one of the driving motors of his theology has in fact been the worry that the American experiment is in deep trouble. It is not that Stanley has been unconcerned about the plight of America, nor that he has thought that Christians have no responsibility to respond to that

2. James McClendon, *Ethics: Systematic Theology*, 2 vols. (Nashville: Abingdon, 1986) 1:230.

3. "The first social task of the church is to help the world know that it is the world. For without the church, the world has no means to know that it is the world." Stanley Hauerwas, "The Gesture of a Truthful Story," *Theology Today* 42 (1985) 182. See also Hauerwas, *Performing the Faith* (Grand Rapids: Brazos, 2004) 56.

4. Stanley Hauerwas, "The Church and Liberal Democracy," in *A Community of Character* (Notre Dame: University of Notre Dame Press, 1981) 74.

5. Stanley Hauerwas, *A Better Hope* (Grand Rapids: Brazos, 2000) 24.

plight. Rather, he has sought to show the work that needs to be done so that American Christians can effectively respond to that plight, and to go about that work.

Christians who have accepted the liberal quarantine of religion into an ostensibly private sphere, who see themselves as individual atoms, freely choosing to join one or another voluntary association, and carefully translating their private religious reasons into acceptably secular reasons, are unfit for meaningful public involvement. Back in 1981, in "The Church and Liberal Democracy," Stanley was particularly concerned to contest "the liberal assumption that a just polity is possible without the people being just."[6] This was to echo civic republican and communitarian thinkers insistent on the necessity for civic virtue if democracies are to flourish. Instead of focusing on laws and procedures that ensure a balance of power and render the conflict among self-interested factions to issue in shared benefit, the civic republican insists that citizens must be capable of setting aside their own narrow self-interest and benefit to those near and dear, capable of wise reflection on and steady support for the common good. Stanley noted that in America today, "people feel their only public duty is to follow their own interests as far as possible, limited only by the rule that we do not unfairly limit others' freedom. As a result we have found it increasingly necessary to substitute procedures and competition for the absence of public virtues."[7] Stanley, though, turned not to civic virtue, whether of a Roman or Machiavellian or Rousseauian vintage, but rather to the church as a school of virtue. For the pretensions of earthly authorities and the potential excesses of our own love of nation can only be held in check by the recognition that "God limits all earthly claims to power."[8] So only a community that recognizes the worship of God as its first task can form genuine virtues and hence form people capable of genuine service to the common good of the societies they inhabit.

Stanley's position thus turns out to have a great deal in common with various perfectionist liberalisms, which give up on the myth of liberal neutrality, note liberalism's commitment to an array of substantive goods, and insist that even within a pluralistic society, there is no substitute for the identification and pursuit of goods in common, in Luke Bretherton's words, "goods in which the good of each is conditional upon the good

6. Hauerwas, "Church and Liberal Democracy," 73.

7. Ibid., 79.

8. Ibid., 85.

of all," "substantive goods in which the flourishing of all is invested."[9] Yet one might wonder whether Stanley's construal of the relationship between Christian virtue and the world sets the stage for an infinite postponement of public engagement. For it is not an easy thing to learn to see and act in the world "not as we want it to be, but as it is, namely, as God's good but fallen creation."[10] We cannot learn to do this in the abstract. Rather, we must be formed within a specific community located in time and place. The world we inhabit is a world shaped by its narratives, its practices. "Our very ability to know what we have done and to claim our behavior as our own," Stanley wrote in The Peaceable Kingdom, "is dependent on the descriptions we learn."[11] While some stories, like that of secular liberalism, tempt us into thinking that we are self-creators, the story Christians tell of God enables us to recognize the giftedness of our existence. Since self-deception, and in particular illusions of independence, are fundamental human realities, the process of becoming formed by a truthful story is slow and painful.[12] Competing narratives surround us and lure us. We must gather in a community whose practices enact the virtues required to live truthfully: "it is from the essential practices of a community," Stanley writes in Performing the Faith, "practices that name the ongoing habits that make it possible for the community to sustain a history, that liturgy forms and reforms our lives."[13] This task of moral formation is never concluded; one can never say, 'okay, now that we've taken care of that task, we are ready to go out and be publicly involved'. So it is understandable that critics might conclude that the task of moral formation has essentially displaced the task of public service.

Actually, Stanley's emphasis on the liturgy as the primary site for Christian formation should itself help to correct this impression. For the rhythm of gathering for worship and being sent forth to serve the world is a neverending cycle. Being sent out is not postponed until one is ready, fully formed, wholly virtuous. Rather, Christians are sent out, resting in God's sustaining grace, and are gathered back in again to confess their failures and be reformed and kneaded again into the Body of Christ.

---

9. Luke Bretherton, Christianity and Contemporary Politics (Oxford: Wiley-Blackwell, 2010) 18.

10. Hauerwas, Peaceable Kingdom, 35.

11. Ibid., 43.

12. Ibid., 47.

13. Hauerwas, Performing the Faith, 156.

Still, Jeffrey Stout's 2004 diagnosis of the rhetorical impact of Stanley's combining of "Yoder's church-world distinction with MacIntyre's antiliberalism" is keen.[14] Stanley, argues Stout, "underestimates the extent to which his heavy-handed use of the term 'liberalism' as an all-purpose critical instrument continually reinforces the impression that total rejection is in fact required."[15] Hence the recurring charges of sectarianism. Stout's own move was not to mount a defense of liberalism, but rather of democracy. And Stanley in recent years has done quite a bit to show that his *basso continuo* commendation of selective social engagement on the part of Christians is more than rhetorical icing on a cake of withdrawal. There is no better example of this than *Christianity, Democracy, and the Radical Ordinary*, co-authored with Romand Coles and consisting largely of conversations between the two. Here we see a willingness to identify shared practices and common goods in a way that neither denies differences nor erects those differences as barriers to working imaginatively together to confront global capitalism and the mega-state. "Democracy" has emerged as a usable term, even if not a first-order theological term, and the liturgical moment of going forth to love and serve neighbor is coming into balance with that of gathering into the particularities of Christian story and practice.

So Stanley's most recent work inhabits a moment of possibility, a moment in which the task of being church can begin to be lived out in an inter- or multi-faith politics of the common good, which does not regard the sustenance of inherited narratives and practices as standing in a zero-sum relationship with practices of invention and crossing-over that forge new forms of fidelity and truthfulness. We are all feeling our way forward here. Take John Milbank and the Radical Orthodoxy movement, for starters. Despite gauntlet-throwing statements proclaiming that the time had come to "to reassert theology as a master discourse," in fact Milbank clearly welcomes cooperation with those of other faiths and of no faith at all, and his critiques of liberalism are aimed not at core democratic commitments but at individualism and a state that is nothing but a shield for individual and collective self-seeking.[16] Radical Orthodoxy declares Enlightenment universalism bankrupt and wholeheartedly embraces a theological

---

14. Jeffrey Stout, *Democracy and Tradition* (Princeton: Princeton University Press, 2004) 148.

15. Ibid.

16. John Milbank, *Theology and Social Theory: Beyond Secular Reason* (Oxford: Blackwell, 1990; 1993) 1, 6; hereafter TST.

particularism in which shared liturgical practices are seen as key to realizing the divine creative purpose of forging community and healing the sin of self-seeking.[17] Yet this does not prevent Milbank from arguing at the same time that there are idolatries not only of "universalizable power" but also of mere particularism, and that a feature common to various religious traditions, reference to a transcendent universal, provides the basis for effective critique of these idolatries.[18] It is, he writes, "precisely the endeavour of the so-called 'axial' religions—Judaism (later Christianity and Islam), Socratic Philosophy and Buddhism" to conceive of the universal as "eternally present yet not fully accessible," "only available as diversely mediated by local pathways."[19]

In some sense there is significant resonance between this project and Stanley's collaboration with Romand Coles. Take another contribution from the Radical Orthodoxy movement, Graham Ward's recent *Politics of Discipleship*, which describes his own project of taking "a religious stand against the materialism engulfing the West" "impolite." Yet Ward also notes that Christians who take up this task of contestation do "not take such a stand alone." Allied forms of resistance can be found "in other faith traditions"; "contestation is not war; it can be honest talk that sets out practices of coexistence and common values."[20] But how can a confessional interfaith politics of the common good be enacted in a way that does not work over time to erode the particularities of faith? Stanley himself is wary of employing generic talk of transcendence. Statements such as that of Milbank, just noted, to the effect that the axial religions share a common reference to a transcendent universal, put him on edge. His allergies to transcendence talk are rooted in his diagnosis of the failures of liberal Protestantism and its search for an essence of Christianity that could survive the eroding acids of the Enlightenment.[21] Liberal theology's attempt to defend the intelligibility and cogency of theological discourse by showing how it responds

---

17. John Milbank, "Postmodern Critical Augustinianism," *Modern Theology* 7.3 (1991) 228.

18. John Milbank, *Being Reconciled: Ontology and Pardon* (London and New York: Routledge, 2003) 174–76.

19. Ibid., 173–74.

20. *The Politics of Discipleship: Becoming Postmaterial Citizens* (Grand Rapids: Baker Academic, 2009) 23; 299.

21. See, e.g., Stanley Hauerwas, "On Keeping Theological Ethics Theological" (1983), in *The Hauerwas Reader*, ed. John Berkman and Michael Cartwright (Durham and London: Duke University Press, 2001) 51–74.

to the human condition was a serious flaw even in thinkers such as H. R. Niebuhr who were committed to keeping theological questions primary for ethical reflection.[22] The language of transcendence is just the sort of generic language that worked to erode the distinctive particularity of Christian theological ethics. Beyond this, Stanley worries that the language of transcendence stands in tension with the fundamentally eschatological orientation of Christian faith: "You can be fairly sure that when transcendence, especially in the name of 'radical monotheism', becomes the hallmark of a theologian's understanding of God, eschatology will disappear all together or, at the very best, have a secondary role."[23] The language of transcendence is static; the language of eschatology is dynamic, a reminder that all of creation is not just, as Radical Orthodoxy proclaims, "suspended" from the transcendent God who holds all of creation in being, but rather that we have our places as players in the radically contingent drama of creation, a drama oriented toward its end in the shared enjoyment of God.[24]

So while Christians and non-Christians alike might conceivably come together around the recognition that "God limits all earthly claims to power," thus checking the pretensions of all earthly authorities, our concern as Christians, Stanley insists, must be to speak as well as we can of a creation redeemed by the cross of Christ, not to worry about whether what we say is going to be acceptable or intelligible to those who do not know Christ.[25] Still, he also affirms that when Christians do this, eschewing both

22. Ibid., 63.

23. Hauerwas, *Performing the Faith*, 16n4.

24. Introduction to *Radical Orthodoxy: A New Theology*, ed. John Milbank, Catherine Pickstock, and Graham Ward (London and New York: Routledge, 1999) 3–4, Catherine Pickstock develops this point about "suspension" in relation to the participatory character of language itself, critiquing modernity's immanentist flattening, in *After Writing: On the Liturgical Consummation of Philosophy* (Oxford: Basil Blackwell, 1998) 47–50.

25. See, for instance, his response to the recent *JRE* focus on his scholarship, and more specifically to my contribution, in which I urge Stanley to declare his allegiance to a comprehensive rather than an exclusive particularism: "Though I think Christians have an obligation to try to understand their non-Christian neighbors, the more important question for me is whether Christians are interesting enough such that those who are not Christian might think it worthwhile to try to understand us" (299), and "The issue . . . is not whether what we have to say as Christians is 'particular' or 'universal' but whether what we have to say can meet the challenges generated both internally and externally by the way the world must be construed given our presumption that all creation has been redeemed by the cross of Christ" (300). "Remembering How and What I Think: A Response to the JRE Articles on Hauerwas," *Journal of Religious Ethics* 40.2 (June 2012) 296–306.

the imposition on others of Christian convictions and the imposition of any would-be universalistic ethic, a space opens up for a "dialogical process of confrontation and reconciliation," for patient, vulnerable practices of listening, relationship-weaving and common dwelling.[26] To act well in a world redeemed by the cross of Christ is not to isolate ourselves from any of our neighbors.

Truthfulness in a Secret Faith?

I have been arguing that Stanley's recent work begins to exemplify how Christians might contribute precisely as Christians to responding to the challenges we face in contemporary American society. Stanley rightly recognizes Luke Bretherton, Eric Gregory, Chuck Mathewes, and Ted Smith as fellow-travelers in this journey.[27] But a recent book by Jonathan Malesic, *Secret Faith in the Public Square*, offers a challenge not just to those who trade Christian commitments for minimalist universalism in order to address public concerns, but also to those who seek to live out their thick Christian identities in public. What are we to make of this provocative interpolation?

Malesic points out that Christians in many regions of the United States, as well as elsewhere in the world, still for many intents and purposes inhabit Christendom. Their public declarations of Christian identity are ways to make friends and influence people, to garner social capital. For example, he notes how important it is for American politicians to be Christians, preferably of some garden variety. And in the business world as well, advertising one's faith can be an avenue to inspiring trust. He argues that this should be cause for concern. It undermines the integrity of Christian faith, rendering it likely that many declarations of faith and exhibitions of Christian commitment are hypocritical. Now, one might argue that the integrity of any form of practical or theoretical commitment is endangered if it becomes a ticket to success, since incentives will exist to adopt that form of life apart from one's own conviction of its goodness and truth. But Malesic's argument goes further. There is something about Christianity in particular that is endangered when it becomes an avenue to power and influence. "Can Christians," he asks, "be witnesses to the hard truths of the gospel in a land where being Christian is a form of political or social

---

26. Stanley Hauerwas and Romand Coles, *Christianity, Democracy, and the Radical Ordinary*, Theopolitical Visions 1 (Eugene, OR: Cascade, 2008) 21.

27. Hauerwas, "Remembering How and What I Think," 303.

capital?"[28] A form of identity that of its own proper nature elicits suspicion, hatred, and persecution, that subjects its bearers to martyrdom, cannot remain itself and become a badge of respectability, let alone a source of status.

Malesic's remedy for this malady is an intriguing one: secrecy. Christians, Malesic advises, ought to conceal their identity in public, so as to ensure that they cannot materially benefit from that identity. Only then, he suggests, can they be sure that their faith is genuine. Christians should hide their light under a bushel after all. "The problem," he tells us, "is not that Christians might bother others with the light from their lamp and so they should keep that light hidden; the problem is that too often in American public life, the light is used to illumine the Christians themselves, bringing glory to precisely the wrong person."[29] For *this* reason, Christian faith should be shrouded in secrecy. Christendom itself has become the locus for Augustine's glittering vice! Christians are allowing the glory of Christian faith to reflect on themselves, rather than ensuring that any glory they receive is referred to God.

These are important observations. It can be difficult for academics, who inhabit a highly distinctive subculture in which Christian faith often elicits distrust or ridicule, to appreciate that public declarations of Christian identity in this country have, generally speaking, absolutely no whiff of martyrdom clinging to them. But Malesic's concerns ring true. In the United States, a public Christian identity is a badge of respectability.

Malesic is keenly aware of our common human tendency to fabricate rationalizations, to find reasons that favor ourselves and our predilections. As psychologist Jonathan Haidt argues in *The Righteous Mind*, "we act like intuitive politicians striving to maintain appealing moral identities in front of our multiple constituencies."[30] If this is the case, then it seems wise to approach the reasons we and others give with a healthy dose of suspicion. Malesic's argument appropriates this hermeneutic of suspicion and offers concealment as a cure. And this might at first blush seem reasonable—if we conceal our actions, we no longer have an audience for these actions, and thus there is no need to be concerned about what that audience thinks about us or our actions. We are freed to perform spontaneous works of love and mercy. However, even if an action or its distinctive Christian meaning

---

28. Jonathan Malesic, *Secret Faith in the Public Square* (Grand Rapids: Brazos, 2009) 15.

29. Ibid., 19.

30. Jonathan Haidt, *The Righteous Mind* (New York: Vintage, 2012) 87–88.

or motivation is somehow concealed from others, the agent is still perform-ing for multiple constituencies—for oneself, of course, and for God. We seek to justify our actions and reactions to ourselves as well as to others. So the hermeneutic of suspicion cuts deeper.[31] It is not simply that we are good at devising rationalizations for our actions, but that we are experts at con-vincing not just others but ourselves. If this is the case, it is hard to see how secrecy can provide a meaningful response to the dangers of rationalization and self-deception. It is not surprising to find Bonhoeffer advocating that Christians should not even know their own goodness, because if they do know it, "it will really be your goodness, and not the goodness of Christ."[32] That is, it will be a form of works-righteousness, done for the sake of being seen; it will not be the love that springs from Christ's grace. So Bonhoeffer argues that genuine deeds of love are hidden from the doer, and spring from what he calls "unconscious Christianity."[33] But how can our deeds be hidden from ourselves and yet meaningfully be said to be our deeds? And how can we consciously cultivate unconscious Christianity?[34]

Stanley, too, has been alert to the ever-present dangers of self-decep-tion. This is a theme that accompanies his sustained concern with discover-ing how we can learn to speak and live truthfully. We can't, he tells us, "know what we are up to and live authentically" unless we avoid self-deception, and we can't avoid self-deception "unless we work at developing the skills required to articulate the shape of our individual and social engagements, or forms of life."[35] Our tendency to self-deception is inveterate; while we

31. And Malesic recognizes this: "theologians," he remarks, "know how easy it is to deceive oneself about one's true motivations for any apparently good action. The herme-neutic of suspicion recognizes that the distance between one's overt and covert motiva-tions is often great, and so this interpretive strategy seeks to uncover unflattering reasons for actions in the public sphere. The suspicious interpreter acknowledges that layers of rationalization and repression often allow us to convince ourselves and others that we are perfectly virtuous" (*Secret Faith*, 20).

32. Dietrich Bonhoeffer, *Discipleship*, volume 4 of *Dietrich Bonhoeffer Works*, ed. Geoffrey B. Kelly and John D. Godsey, trans. Barbara Green and Reinhard Krauss (Min-neapolis: Fortress, 2003) 150–51; quoted in Malesic, *Secret Faith*, 145.

33. Bonhoeffer, *Letters and Papers from Prison*, enlarged ed., ed. Eberhard Bethge (New York: Touchstone, 1997) 380; quoted in Malesic, *Secret Faith*, 147.

34. Malesic acknowledges that the effort might seem to be self-defeating: "the para-dox is that it takes discipline and self-reflection to become unreflective about one's faith," *Secret Faith*, 147.

35. Hauerwas, "Self-Deception and Autobiography: Reflections on Speer's Inside the Third Reich," (1974), with David Burrell, in *The Hauerwas Reader*, 200.

profess and aspire to sincerity, we "deliberately allow certain engagements to go unexamined, quite aware that areas left unaccountable tend to cater to self-interest."[36] We identify with our societal roles without spelling out their significance. We need to be trained to be conscious of what we are doing and who we are. But the spelling out of our commitments also requires courage, since it can require a painful confrontation with our own sinfulness.[37] We are capable of telling our own story truthfully only in relation to basic stories and master images in relation to which we situate ourselves. And "Christians claim to find the skill to confess the evil that we do in the history of Jesus Christ."[38] The Enlightenment encouraged us to think that we free ourselves from self-deception insofar as we free ourselves of particularistic stories, particularly those we have not autonomously chosen. But Stanley argues that examination of our habits, consciousness with respect to our social roles, the ability to stand back from and spell out our commitments, is made possible not by detachment from master narratives, but rather by attachment to a truthful story. The formation of a self by such a narrative is a practical, communal manner. And within such a community of shared practice, the community of the church, the task of self-examination is not an individual matter. Rather, we bear a responsibility to confront one another's sinfulness and to confess our own sinfulness to one another. We cannot overcome self-deception, then, on our own, but only together, as a community of people schooled in the narrative of our giftedness, fallenness, and forgiveness. This was back in 1973; generic talk of "master narratives" and "truthful stories" is later thrown out, but not formation by the truthful story of God in Christ. Indeed, in the latest issue of the JRE, Stanley, responding to, and I almost want to say foxtrotting gracefully away from, Santurri's critique, sounds this theme once again: "I am sure Santurri is right," he says, "to suggest that 'both natural and biblical theology are liable to sinful distortion in a fallen world, but that possibility does not show that either is intrinsically deficient.' If *any* kind of theology at all is liable to sinful distortion, the answer lies not with better theology, of whatever kind. Stanley goes on: "People make a difference. That means the question cannot be avoided of what kind of formation was necessary to

36. Hauerwas, "Self-Deception," 201.

37. This was Stanley's take on self-deception back in 1973. In 2004 he was still insisting that "nothing is more important for the world than for Christians to learn to confess our sins," *Performing the Faith*, 25.

38. Hauerwas, "Self-Deception," 219.

produce a Karl Barth who could see the Nazis for what they were."[39] Stanley is not interested in a reductive account of truth as warranted assertability; such an account would be a performative self-contradiction, for one thing, and could not possibly capture the logic of Christian claims about God and the world any more than of our humblest truth claims. But he *is* worried that claims about general moral truths and universal moral laws are a favorite hiding-place for pride: as he concludes in his response to Santurri: "Wittgenstein (and Barth) provides the therapies that hopefully help us avoid the pride Santurri rightly identifies as sin." And again, we must be *formed* to see and name pride; the best theorizing of whatever variety may be necessary, but can never be sufficient.

To confront one another's sinfulness is to engage in a practice of reason-giving, to ask others to give reasons for their actions and commitments and to call into question the adequacy of the reasons we are given. It is an exercise in accountability. In lieu of secrecy, we are to call ourselves and one another into the light of day; in lieu of actions without reasons (Bonhoeffer's deeds that interpret themselves), we are to demand an extra dose of reason-giving. But here we confront another problem. For our inveterate tendency toward self-deception is not simply individual but communal. We are, as Haidt puts it, less selfish than we are "groupish." We favor our political, ethnic, regional, religious groups, and our identity is deeply bound up with our identification with these groups. So, for instance, people typically do not choose political candidates or policies according to what will benefit them the most. We look not for what is in it for us, but what is in it for our group.[40] We are not rational choice actors. There is an angelic side to this feature of human nature. Through our identification with our groups, we are drawn beyond ourselves, able to transcend self-interest. We find in our groups something higher than ourselves that is worth living for and even worth dying for. But there is also a demonic side to our groupishness. Much of the evil that we do is in service of our groups. We dismiss or demonize outsiders, and "isolate ourselves within cocoons of like-minded individuals."[41] This of course enhances our confirmation biases; if the exchange of reasons with others is critical to our capacity to seek truth rather than simply rationalize what we already believe, surrounding

---

39. Stanley Hauerwas, "Niebuhr One More Time: A Response to Santurri," *Journal of Religious Ethics* 41:3 (2013) 549.

40. Haidt, *Righteous Mind*, 100.

41. Ibid., 363.

ourselves with those who think just the way we do can render the process of reason-giving simply an exercise in reinforcing our convictions. Similarly, we accept norms for behavior that are operative within our own cocoons, and justify our actions according to those norms, those expectations. In a community that is insulated from contact with those outside, there will be little call to reflect on the justifiability of the way we do things.

This suggests that it is vital that our practices of reason-giving extend beyond whatever cocoons we find ourselves nestling in, if we are effectively to confront our tendencies toward self-deception. It is necessary that we be formed in truthfulness, not just theoretically instructed, but formation is also powerfully insulating, deafening us to just the critiques we most need to hear. So formation for truthfulness must be accompanied by, indeed constituted by, the best truth-seeking practices we have. Stanley recognizes this, but I want to underscore the full breadth of its ramifications. We must learn to regard the existence of others and their differences as a gift, he insists, one that allows us to discern and test our own roles in our community's story. This is the case even if the existence of others is naturally experienced as threatening to myself and my identity, insofar as it reminds me that I could have been other than I am. "The truthfulness of the adventure tale is thus partly tested by how it helps me negotiate the existence of the other both as threat and as a gift for the existence of my own story."[42] So if Christian stories become an excuse for insulating ourselves from non-Christian or secular others, we are in trouble. We have then found our identity within a story that reinforces rather than penetrates our individual and communal self-deceptions. Stanley tells us that being the church "entails being a community capable of being a critic to every human pretension."[43] The church can be a critic to every human pretension insofar as its loyalty is to God, who limits all earthly claims to power. But our loyalty to God rather than human pretension cannot be sustained within cocoons that inevitably are woven together with human pretensions. So the church's gift to the world of truthfulness is a gift that can be given only insofar as the church does not simply show itself forth to the world but also speaks with the world, asking for and giving reasons in a risky and imaginative process of plural particularities.

42. Hauerwas, "Character, Narrative, and Growth in the Christian Life," (1980), in *Hauerwas Reader*, 250.

43. Hauerwas, *Peaceable Kingdom*, xviii.

Now, one might object that exchanging reasons with non-Christian others cannot possibly aid us in being truthful, since these others fail to recognize that only a life of discipleship to Jesus, only a life that shares in Trinitarian ecstasy, can be truthful, and that understanding of truthfulness is intelligible only with reference to its significance within the embodied life of the church. To be sure, it is not always clear how we can exchange reasons with all comers. Stanley notes, for instance, that while those who believe in God and those who do not often assume that they know what the others mean when they say "God," they do not, since "Christians believe that we learn to use the word 'God' only through worship and prayer to the One we address as Father, Son, and Spirit."[44] We are never done with learning the story that allows us to say "God." Since meaning is normed by use, speech by practices, we cannot exchange reasons with those with whom we do not share practices. But this just means that we will do better to begin by talking about some arena in which we *do* share practices—about bricklaying, or baseball, or homelessness—and sometimes that we must commit ourselves to the *construction* of shared practices—and that we would do better not to *begin* some conversations by talking about "God," even if we confess God as the one to whom all conversations point and in whom all conversations end. All human beings recognize that the stilling of hunger is good; food sustains life, food is good, the life it sustains is good. Not only do we all share practices of eating, we all share practices of reason-giving surrounding eating, practices in which certain judgments are implicit.[45] Do I know what a member of some remote cannibal tribe means when she says "food"? Does she know what I, a member of the Body of Christ, sustained by his body and blood, mean when I say "food"? Surely, we spend our lifetimes learning how we need to speak of the Body of Christ in order to say "food" well. Yet all of our near and distant neighbors understand what it is to share a meal, so a lifetime of reason-giving can rather easily get off the ground, even if it never concludes. Stanley has said that learning how to say "God" forces us to be "honest with ourselves" about the fact that we are "creatures destined to die," our lives but a flicker.[46] I think he is right about this. But it is also true that this is a simple truth that every human being

---

44. Hauerwas, *Hannah's Child*, 236.

45. John Bowlin, "Nature's Grace: Aquinas and Wittgenstein on Natural Law and Moral Knowledge," in *Grammar and Grace: Reformulations of Aquinas and Wittgenstein*, ed. Jeffrey Stout and Robert Macswain (London: SCM, 2004) 163.

46. Stanley Hauerwas, "Love," in *Working With Words: On Learning to Speak Christian* (Eugene, OR: Cascade, 2011) 6.

knows, as well as a truth that every human being spends a lifetime learning, a lifetime up to the moment of one's own death. This world is still God's good creation, after all.

We see this commitment to exchanging reasons with others reflected in John Howard Yoder's defense of democracy. First, Yoder argued that the fact that Christians were called to servanthood did not mean that they should not ask others for reasons and hold them responsible for living up to the commitments they themselves have made. He notes, in particular, that while Christians are not to play the game of "rulers-making-a-case for-their-benevolence," they may and should use this game as leverage for critique. "If the ruler claims to be my benefactor, and he always does, then that claim provides me as his subject with the language I can use to call him to be more humane in his ways of governing me and my neighbors. . . . I am quite free to use his language to reach him."[47] So Christians are to hold others responsible for their commitments, asking them to account for their actions in light of their own beliefs and values. This does not mean that the faith community speaks to itself in the same way as it speaks "to the nations." Diverse semantic frames are the norm, not the exception; reason-giving is always radically context dependent.

In addition to this negative case in favor of democracy, Yoder also articulated a more positive case, which "properly arises in those places where their numbers, or their virtues, or their friends, or their good luck should give to Christians a chance for positive model building."[48] Here the church is offered as a model for the civil commonwealth, in the specific sense of offering a model of a community in which all are free to speak and all are to listen critically to what is spoken; "if that is the way divine truth is to be articulated in the words of our world, then those who have learned those skills of listening critically and speaking prophetically should be able as well to apply them to debates about human justice."[49] The ongoing dialectical, communal process of discerning God's Word is lived out both for itself and as a model for all discernment. This is, in fact, one instantiation of the logic of servanthood—we do not seek to manipulate others by strategically or tantalizingly concealing and revealing various truths or commitments. Rather, we exchange reasons, we hold others accountable and allow them

47. John Howard Yoder, *The Priestly Kingdom* (Notre Dame: University of Notre Dame Press, 1984) 158.

48. Ibid., 166.

49. Ibid.

to hold us accountable, because to do so is to acknowledge their dignity as creatures made in the image of God. What was new as democracy emerged out of Puritan and Quaker meetings, Yoder argues, "was that peculiar commitment to the dignity of the adversary or the interlocutor which alone makes dialogue an obligation, and which can be rooted only in some transcendent claim."[50]

There are plenty of echoes of this Yoderian point in Stanley's writings over the years, and indeed it stands at the heart of his understanding of Christian nonviolence. It is not accidental that Yoder, with his emphasis on vulnerable engagement, looms large in Stanley's collaboration with Romand Coles. "All genuine politics," Stanley tells us, "that is, politics in the sense of conversation necessary for a people to discover the goods they have in common—are nonviolent. Rather than denying the political, nonviolence requires that we become political by forcing us to listen to the other rather than destroy them."[51] To deny a priori the possibility of understanding, to insist a priori on unintelligibility, is itself a kind of violence. Over against this, we are called to trust in the possibility of discovering goods in common, which itself is a trust that even a fallen and divided world is still the beloved world of God's creation.

I promised at the outset to take up two points. And here I am, drawing to a close, with the second point apparently untouched. I have tried to underscore Stanley's acknowledgement that truthfulness can be nourished only insofar as we are prepared to listen not just to our own weakest members, but also to those who regard themselves as quite foreign to the Body of Christ. As Pope Francis said in a recent interview, "Between a Church that goes into the street and gets into an accident and a Church that is sick with self-referentiality, I have no doubts in preferring the first."[52] Truthfulness cannot grow inside a cocoon. But what of McClendon's point, that the church-world distinction passes through the heart of every believer and every churchly practice? What I want to say here can be said quickly, since it returns us to what I have already said. Sometimes it is easier to listen to those who regard themselves as quite foreign to the Body of Christ than it is to listen to those who compose that Body differently than we do. The

50. Ibid., 168.

51. Hauerwas, "On Being a Church Capable of Addressing a World at War: A Pacifist Response to the United Methodist Pastoral In Defense of Creation" (1988), in *Hauerwas Reader*, 454.

52. Antonio Spadaro, "A Big Heart Open to God," September 30, 2013, *America*, http://americamagazine.org/pope-interview.

church is not one cocoon but many, and our reason-giving practices easily become confined to the like-minded, to those who construe our greatest challenges and greatest opportunities in the way we do. Groupishness reproduces itself at many levels, and even those schooled together in the narrative of our giftedness, fallenness, and forgiveness, and fed together at altar and common table, can find it hard to allow their self-deceptions to be pierced by one another. We are still left asking one another "whose story?" "which narrative?" and constantly struggling to discern the shape of Christ, of God with us.

Tradition cannot be sustained passively or by turning inward: "even the wisdom of the last generation," Stanley has written, "fails to serve us as it did our fathers, since we have received it without a struggle."[53] This notion of storytellers who sustain the truthfulness of their story only as they open it up to reason-giving exchanges with other storytellers—and with those we feel sure are distorting our story—may leave us with a bit of a sense of anomie. So it is worth reminding ourselves that Stanley never promised that the Christian story would give us comforting security. "If the true God were to provide us with a saving story, it would have to be one that we found continually discomforting."[54] Stanley, you have been a good and faithful servant of that discomforting and saving story. For that we are all in your debt.

53. Hauerwas, "Self-Deception and Autobiography," *Reader*, 216.
54. Ibid.

Response to Jennifer Herdt's "Truthfulness and Continual Discomfort"

Charlie Pinches

JENNIFER HERDT HAS PRESENTED us with a gracious response to Stanley Hauerwas's long and distinguished scholarly career, a response that centers on the church-world relation, and so on the way in which Stanley believes Christians should address the political worlds in which they find themselves. In what follows, I will try briefly to summarize how she handles this important topic, and then offer a few critical points with hopes for further engagement.

But first, notice that even though Jennifer tells us she was never a student of Stanley's, she cannot resist offering a personal story about her encounter with "the brash, foul-mouthed Texan" who often announced his pacifism in provocative ways, consonant with his self-description that he was "by disposition not much inclined to non-violence."[1] There is, after all, something irresistible about a Stanley story. Moreover, since I *was* a student of Stanley's, I have a much deeper (and juicier) fund to draw on in this regard. So let me also begin with a story about the foul-mouthed Texan and non-violence.

Early in my teaching career I invited Stanley to speak to a large group of soon-to-be college freshmen at Hendrix College in Arkansas. These students had been classified "gifted" by the Arkansas state government, which mainly meant they had become jaded before their time. In his morning lecture Stanley had been characteristically Hauerwas, full of potential offense. Many were enticed to return for the Q and A session in the afternoon. He

1. See chapter 2 above, 26.

43

began that session with a few comments about his topic, war, then announced to the students that as a Christian he believed faithful discipleship of Jesus required pacifism. After which he said: "I tell you this because, as you well know by now, I am a violent son-of-a-bitch and I need you to hold me to my confession." And then he opened the floor for questions.

I will return to this story, for I think it shows something important about how Stanley has taught those of us in the church to relate to the world. For her part, Herdt builds her response to Stanley's approach to church-world relations mainly around this statement: "even if it is indeed the case that the world cannot know it to be the world without the help of the church, it is also the case that the church cannot help us to speak truthfully unless it speaks not just to, but also with the world."[2] I think she thinks that Stanley generally agrees with this statement, although perhaps sometimes less enthusiastically and consistently than she might wish.

Jennifer moves to a consideration of Stanley's emphasis that church discipleship and polity should form Christians in the skills necessary to live truthfully—and so will assist any society they inhabit to know justice and truth. She notes that this is not necessarily a recipe for "withdrawal from social and political involvement," although it does press Christians to be, as Stanley himself says, "politically involved *as Christians*." This is especially true in America, where we are strongly tempted to make the subject of Christian ethics in America America rather than that church. Despite this, however, Herdt insists that "one of the driving motors of [Hauerwas's] theology has in fact been the worry that the American experiment is in deep trouble."[3] (I think this is not quite accurate, but more on that in a minute.)

Herdt draws a parallel between what she takes to be Stanley's position and "various perfectionist liberalisms" which turn away from liberal proceduralism toward virtue—acknowledging that we need good people to make a good society. Unlike these liberalisms, though, Hauerwas accents not society's but rather the church's role as a school for virtue. A difficulty with this accent for Herdt is that the formation in virtue in the church could, by its own logic, go on indefinitely, "an infinite postponement of public engagement."[4] This is where Jennifer rehearses a concern expressed by her own teacher, Jeffrey Stout, about the profoundly negative effect of Hauerwas's combination of "Yoder's church-world distinction with

2. Ibid.

3. Ibid., 27.

4. Ibid., 29.

Macintyre's antiliberalism."[5] She calls Stout's point "*keen.*" However, Herdt thinks Hauerwas has exonerated himself more recently, particularly in his collaboration with Rom Coles on democracy.[6] To Herdt's credit, she does not take this recent dialogue with Coles' democracy as aberration; despite widespread belief to the contrary, Stanley has always cared about engaging the world. How to do this, though, is a delicate thing. "We are all feeling our way forward here," she says.[7] I like that. Indeed, she puts the problem before us well: "[H]ow can a confessional interfaith politics of the common good be enacted in such a way that it does not work over time to erode the particularities of faith?"[8]

Jennifer goes on to entertain the possibility of Christians keeping their faith a secret in the current American environment where a residual Christendom yet rules the day. Here she appreciates the emphasis Stanley has placed on the dangers of self-deception, but wants to be sure this is extended to the self-deceptive "groupishness" we can fall prey to, perhaps especially in the church. She lauds Stanley's accent on regarding "the existence of others and their differences as a gift,"[9] one that can help us test our own community's story and challenge us to give reasons for what we do and love as we interact with those outside of our group. Here she opens the possibility, which she thinks Stanley affirms, that in such interactions we will discover "goods in common." These might be as basic as "*food*" which we all share—even if Christians also proceed to speak, perhaps oddly to others, of the body of Christ as food.

Interestingly, Herdt thinks John Yoder actually showed us something about how the church might engage the world on the topic of democracy. Yoder, of course, taught Hauerwas much about Christian non-violence. Building on this, Herdt cites Stanley's own words about how a commitment to non-violence forces us to listen to others, and then adds: "To deny a priori the possibility of understanding, to insist a priori on unintelligibility, is itself a kind of violence. Over against this we are called to trust in the possibility of discovering goods in common, which itself is a trust that even a fallen and divided world is still the beloved world of God's creation."[10]

5. Ibid., 30.

6. Hauerwas and Coles, *Christianity, Democracy and the Radical Ordinary.*

7. See above, 30.

8. Ibid., 31.

9. Ibid., 38..

10. Ibid., 41.

⍊

Now, by way of critical response, it seems to me that Jennifer's criticism of Stanley's political engagement, muted and respectful as it is, falls within what is by far the most common criticism of his work: the specter of *sectarianism*. People are still worried that Stanley wants a church that somehow holds itself back from political engagement with the world. Of course Stanley has addressed this many times; its recurrence must indicate something. Either somebody isn't talking clearly enough, or else somebody else isn't listening . . . or maybe a little of both.

I think Herdt may not have been listening so well on a couple of points. First, she alleges that Stanley's theology is driven, at least in part, by his worry that the "American experiment" is in deep trouble. I do not believe Stanley has ever used the term "the American Experiment" in any way other than as parody. It implies American exceptionalism, which Stanley has always eschewed. In 1988 he criticized Max Stackhouse's suggestion that "America is the great experiment in 'constructive Protestantism,'" noting that, for Stackhouse, to "support democracy became a means of supporting Christianity, and vice versa."[11] When they proceed this way, American Christians, like Jeremiah's lusty stallions, throw themselves at democracy or America or liberalism as if it were the gospel. As Stanley says twelve years later, "The object of my criticism of liberalism has never been liberals, but rather to give Christians renewed confidence in the convictions that make our service intelligible. From my perspective the problem is not liberalism but the assumption on the part of many Christians that they must become liberals . . . to be of service in America."[12] As he implies, liberal presumptions have so thoroughly infused all of our lives, Christians included, that Christians have forgotten who they are and whom they serve. Here Christ makes the difference. Accenting this difference, Hauerwas has articulated a genuine alternative for American Christians, or other Christians who are tempted to mistake the nation-state for the church. To show the difference clearly, Hauerwas has needed to accent how his alternative is not just another recipe for cooking the same old liberal stew.

I suspect this had something to do with the flash of excitement Jennifer describes feeling when she first read Hauerwas. I don't know if this was before or after she went to study with Jeffrey Stout, but plainly his criticism

11. Hauerwas, *Christian Existence Today*, 176.
12. Hauerwas, *Better Hope*, 24.

46

of Stanley's work continues to have purchase for her. To be sure, *Democracy and Tradition* (2004) was an interesting and important book. It also left a large pile of dung on Stanley's doorstep. While Stout attacks three so-called "traditionalists"—MacIntyre, Milbank, and Hauerwas—Stanley justifiably later claimed that "Stout's criticism of Milbank and MacIntyre serve to introduce his critique of my position."[13] While I liked Stout's book, it also seemed wrong, even unfair to me, especially when criticizing Stanley and his students. I was therefore somewhat surprised to hear Stanley praise it. "Put bluntly," he says, "this is a position with which we Christians not only can, but should want to, do business with. Stout does try to give an account of democratic life that is not in the first place state theory. I am extremely sympathetic with that project."[14]

This comment is revealing. Stout did what Stanley wants people to do if they set about to interact with his theological writing: he declared clearly that he claims a particular tradition, the tradition of democracy, and engaged, even attacked, Stanley from within it. *This is interesting!* The same dynamic informs the book Jennifer likes so well with Rom Coles. As the authors say in the preface, "This book is about listening. We have had to learn to listen to one another. . . Listening not only takes time, but it also requires a trained vulnerability that does not come easily. Vulnerability means that our life is not under our control, which means we must learn to trust others if we are not only to survive but flourish. Such a politics is in sharp contrast to the politics of fear that characterizes current American life."[15]

In these comments and others, it seems to me that Stanley shows Jennifer exactly what she seems to want when she speaks at the end of her paper about the need to discover goods in common. So, one might ask, what is the problem? Or, to return to an earlier question, why does the sectarian objection still persist (even a little bit) in Herdt?

I have meant to suggest that the persistence of this objection has partly to do with people not listening, but I think there is more. I don't think Stanley has yet fully articulated his vision of engagement with the world in such a way that it goes beyond his personally expressed sentiments about what he has learned from others or how he cherishes them as friends. When we hear stories of friendship between Stanley and the likes of Rom Coles and Jeff Stout and read their honest debates, or when we tell Stanley stories like

---

13. Hauerwas, *Performing the Faith*, 223.

14. Ibid., 224.

15. Hauerwas and Coles, *Christianity, Democracy, and the Radical Ordinary*, 5.

the one I told earlier of his engaging students in Arkansas, we can chalk these up to his extraordinary personality. Only Stanley would say and do such things! We talk this way partly to honor Stanley, marveling at how unique he is, but I think this can become dangerous if we do not also say more. If we are gathered here today only to honor a personality, what are we to do when it is gone? It should not be embarrassing to say in the presence of this man who has so consistently urged us to speak truthfully that a party for his retirement (particularly on All-Saints Day) cannot but remind us that he will someday leave not only the classroom, but this world. What then?

So we must return to the theological argument. Jennifer mentions Stout's observation that Stanley can't combine Yoder's church-world distinction with Macintyre antiliberalism without adopting a troublesome dualism. She calls this observation *keen*—but I cannot agree. In fact, I think Stanley's life and work has shown us that we need both. In response to Stout on the Yoder-MacIntyre binary, Stanley makes a number of cogent points, but I think skips the most important. I think we should say, simply, that Yoder is largely right about how and why the church should avoid the temptation of Constantinianism, and Macintyre is largely right about how and why the university and other intuitions that serve the common good should avoid the temptation of liberalism. Put differently, if we only had MacIntyre, we would not know very well how to speak about what goes on, or should go on, in the church; but if we only had Yoder, we would not know well how to speak about what goes on, or should go on, in places like the university that serve the common good. As I suspect, in Stanley's engagement socially and politically, and also within the university (for example in his exchanges with colleagues like Stout and Coles), he has depended on Macintyre—and with Macintyre the tradition from Aquinas of the virtues and the natural law—much more than he has depended on Yoder. However, he has not consistently articulated his dependence in this area, tending instead to repair to Yoderian moves.

Near the end of her paper Jennifer takes up John Yoder's engagement with democracy as a sort of model. Yet it seems to me that Yoder's position lacks the urgency she hopes for. Yoder is quite specific in the article she quotes that he believes the question "What is the best form of government?" is a Constantinian question.[16] Tyrants everywhere offer claims of benevolence to their subjects, and so too the elites who run democratic

16. Yoder, *Priestly Kingdom*, 154.

societies like ours. In any regime Christians should hold governments to their promises. In "democracies" it is somewhat more likely that Christians will find the skills they have acquired in the church to help out in the business of governance, for example in conflict resolution; if so, they might legitimately serve it in some limited way.

Yoder's point is well and good, but again, it lacks the urgency or intimacy of Coles and Hauerwas's pledge, just quoted, about how we must learn to trust one another if we are not only to survive but to flourish. While Yoder tells us from within the church why it is okay to serve in governance if it suits us, he cannot tell us why we *need* to reach out in friendship to those in our universities or towns or neighborhoods who are not also members of the church in any form other than witness. Put bluntly, Hauerwas cannot get from Yoder an account of the service to the common good that he has tirelessly offered throughout his long career, a service, essentially, of *political friendship*. And this is why he needs MacIntyre, and the long tradition that comes with him.

Let me truncate my point by simply quoting from Fr. Herbert McCabe: "beneath the notion of the natural law [is] the idea that there are things becoming and unbecoming to human beings as such just in virtue of their nature, just in virtue of the kind of animals they are. The idea of natural law depends, as I see it, on being somehow able to see humanity itself on the analogy of a society bound together in friendship."[17]

Early in his career Stanley was given strong reason by misrepresentations of the day to distrust and avoid natural law talk, and his discovery of Yoder only added to this. But I do not think he (or those of us who follow) can fully appropriate the insights of the likes of Aquinas and Macintyre without some articulation along the lines of what McCabe sketches here. Moreover, such an articulation will help us better understand the deep importance of what Stanley has personally modeled for us so well, a friendship that extends beyond church, but also informs life in the church—where it reaches its true supernatural end in friendship with God.

When Stanley confessed his pacifism and his Christian discipleship to my students in Arkansas he offered a witness to them about what the gospel might do and mean as it captures the heart and soul of a man. But he also did something else. When he challenged them to hold him to his non-violent confession he extended to them the hand of friendship and,

17. Herbert McCabe, *The Good Life: Ethics and the Pursuit of Happiness* (London: Continuum, 2005) 13.

indeed, modeled for them, foul-mouthed Texan style, how that friendship might work in the universities to which they were headed. The friendship included this: all of us, Christian or otherwise, need one another to hold us accountable to the truths we claim and the traditions and histories we represent. As Coles and Hauerwas suggest, minus this friendship we will be overrun with fear and suspicion, and the political darkness will deepen.

Stanley Hauerwas has worked his whole life long to make friends with us all—and look how many of us have come to honor him. We will honor him more if we keep our friendships—the very ones he has taught us to form and cherish—with us after this gathering, even after his service is ended at this university or on this earth.

3

Anne and the Difficult Gift of Stanley
Hauerwas's Church

Jonathan Tran

PAULA AND STANLEY, READING from Colossians, "For you, we always thank God, the Father of our Lord Jesus Christ, for we have witnessed your faith in Christ Jesus and of the love you have for all the saints, because of the hope laid up for you in heaven" (Col 1:3–4). Stanley, your work has been such that going forward we will not be able to tell the story of twentieth-century American theology without mentioning your pivotal role in it, a reality about which I'm sure you don't care; in that case we should simply say: for many of us, twentieth-century theology came to matter because of you, and for that we are grateful.

I don't have time this morning to give a full overview of Professor Hauerwas's work, if such an enterprise is even possible, but only to key in on a particular feature of it. The occasion does oblige me to at least name that broader corpus, and so before I turn to the particular feature that concerns me today, here goes. In this *Good Company* of people who know about *Performing the Faith*, regarding the deep and wide influence of Stanley Hauerwas, one need only say: *Working with Words* within *The State of the University* and now *Approaching the End*, Stanley Hauerwas, a.k.a. *Hannah's Child*, has been a *Suffering Presence* for *A Better Hope*, as he, *Without Apology*, calls *Resident Aliens* back to *A Community of Character* that he understands as the *Cross-Shattered Church*. (Oh I'm only getting started, for ask any *Hauerwas Reader*, including my good friend *Matthew*, a *Companion to Christian Ethics*, Stanley hasn't exactly been *Naming the Silences* as he's written on every conceivable topic from *Christianity, Democracy, and the Radical Ordinary* to *Wilderness Wanderings*.) Hauerwas, now *Growing Old in Christ With the Grain of the Universe, Dispatches from the Front* those who claim *War and the American Difference*, often driving them to *God, Medicine, and Suffering*. Preaching *The Wisdom of the Cross* in *Dissent from the Homeland*, Professor Hauerwas heralds *Character and the Christian Life* as the seat of the *Vision and Virtue* necessary to ask questions like "*Should War Be Eliminated?*" praying, with *Prayers Plainly Spoken*, that God would *Sanctify Them in the Truth-Fulness and Tragedy* because he believes that *Schooling Christians* on *The Truth About God* entails, *After Christendom, Christian Existence Today Unleashing the Scriptures Against the Nations* indeed *Where Resident Aliens Live Gently in a Violent World* as *The Peaceable Kingdom*. Good grief, for a person who has authored so many books about what the church does, you sure don't have a lot of active verbs in your titles.

Now that I have summarized all of Professor Hauerwas's theology, I turn to a much more specific concern—that is, to some questions raised by his extraordinary *Hannah's Child: A Theologian's Memoir*, significant parts of which chronicle his marriage to Anne Hauerwas and her difficulties with bipolar illness. Notre Dame's Gerald McKenny raises one of the most poignant questions asked of the 2010 memoir. In a private letter he gave Hauerwas permission publicly to respond to, Professor McKenny asks, "Is Anne one of the strange members of the Christian community whose presence with us teaches us how to be Christians, or is she the surd that resists your story, refusing to be assimilated into it and therefore reminding you of the limits of any account of Christian discipleship, including yours? My sense is she is the latter and you did not really let her play that role."[1] By using the word "surd" McKenny means to impress on us the likelihood that Anne Hauerwas, like an irrational number or a sound for which we cannot account or an event devoid of meaning, does not fit the story Stanley Hauerwas wants to tell about God. Narrate that story with Anne in it and it will not add up, it will leave things unaccounted for, it will not make sense.

1. Stanley Hauerwas, *Hannah's Child: A Theologian's Memoir* (Grand Rapids: Eerdmans, 2012) 303.

Hauerwas sees McKenny here suggesting, "I may well not be aware of how profoundly Anne's life stands as an intractable argument against my theology." It is no wonder that McKenny confesses he raises his question "with fear and trembling."

In a 2011 lecture series reflecting on mental illness, Hauerwas phrased McKenny's challenge this way: "[McKenny] observes that I have written well about how we are able to understand those we label as mentally handicapped in Christian terms, but I do not nor is it possible for me to do the same with one suffering bipolar illness."[2] At those lectures, Fuller's Nancy Murphy, a long-time friend and reader of Hauerwas, took the question further. She gamely quoted from the 1977 *Truthfulness and Tragedy* where Hauerwas seemed to admit that there were indeed difficulties that cannot be "assimilated" into God's redemption, and so therefore prove problematic for the account of Christian discipleship for which Hauerwas has become famous.

Together, I interpret McKenny and Murphy as saying a couple of things: that Anne Hauerwas is a surd to the story Hauerwas tells of the church, and that Anne Hauerwas is a surd to the story Hauerwas tells about *himself* insofar as he tells his story as a story of the church. To this intertwined story—Hauerwas's story as a story of the church through which he finds so "interesting" that he has been made Christian—does Anne remain outside, a fact that would render the story's other facts questionable?[3] In the following, I would like to take McKenny's challenge in two parts. First, is there something about gathered communal life that necessarily excludes the possibility of full assimilation? Second, is Stanley in *Hannah's Child*, to use language from *Truthfulness and Tragedy*, "self-deceived"? Has Professor Hauerwas's vision of the gathered church not accounted for how communal life strands and even abandons some and so bears a difficulty that undermines that vision? In the published version of these comments, which we now have as the Afterword to the new edition of *Hannah's Child*, Professor Hauerwas responds to McKenny's challenge, "I quite frankly do not know." He concludes "The best I can do in answer to McKenny's challenge is to

---

2. 2011 Fuller Symposium on the Integration of Faith and Psychology "Reflections on God and Mental Illness", https://itunes.apple.com/itunes-u/reflections-on-god-mental/id421939843.

3. Hauerwas, *Hannah's Child*, 284.

repeat what John Westerhoff said to me when I claimed after Anne's suicide attempt that she was absolutely alone: 'No, she is not. God is with her.'" [4]

Celebrating the remarkable work and life of our teacher, colleague, friend, and brother Stanley Hauerwas, I would like for us to think through this challenge, about whether Anne Hauerwas is a difficulty for the story Professor Hauerwas tells about himself and the church, a story we, or I should say I, so desperately want to believe to be true, though perhaps is not true given the character of this difficulty. I take this question—initially a question about self-deception and finally a question about the limits of the goodness of the Gospel, and therefore for any Hauerwasian worth her salt about the limits of the goodness of the church—as one that demands asking. The fact that this question is raised most hauntingly by the *life* of Stanley Hauerwas even though his *work* has pressed it going on five decades now, is surely God's good humor in showing us once again that *ad hominem* arguments do indeed matter for Christian theology.

Part I: The Difficult Gift of Anne Hauerwas

In that Afterword to *Hannah's Child*, Professor Hauerwas turns to the philosopher Stanley Cavell in order to treat themes of pain raised by life with Anne.[5] He finds Cavell helpful for identifying the kind of difficulty we confront in the mentally ill, those who have been ruled out of our world and the pain of realizing they have been ruled out. For Cavell, there is a small difference—a difference that sits on a pin's head of grammar—between being in and being out, and one's fate has everything to do with one's ability to mean what *we* mean when one says what *we* say.[6] For Hauerwas, part of the difficulty is that the very resources we have for understanding our lives are not available for understanding the lives of the mad. He writes, "The mentally ill may have shattered lives, but how that is different from the way sin distorts our ability to comprehend who we are as God's creatures is not clear."[7] And so vice versa, because the proximity between the ability and the inability to mean what we say, between being in and being out, between

4. Hauerwas, *Hannah's Child*, 305.

5. Ibid., 293.

6. See Stanley Cavell's *Must We Mean What We Say?* (Cambridge: Cambridge University Press, 2002), *The Claim of Reason: Wittgenstein, Skepticism, Morality, and Tragedy* (Oxford: Oxford University Press, 1979), and *Pursuits of Happiness: The Hollywood Comedy of Remarriage* (Cambridge: Harvard University Press, 1984).

7. Hauerwas, *Hannah's Child*, 293.

normality and madness, is closer than we care to admit. This proximity makes appellations of "madness" all the more terrifying since being close but not inside another's world means one just might have the capacity to recognize one has been ruled out.[8]

Richard Fleming refers to Cavell's ordinary language thought as a philosophy of constraints and entailments, for it is by the logical constraint and entailment of our words that we can mean anything at all. Like Cavell before him, Fleming draws on J. L. Austin's essay "A Plea for Excuses" regarding "what we should say when, and so why and what we should mean by it."[9] For Austin, language carries on without excuse; its users presume its sufficiency, believing that the world language provides is indeed the world: when we say "world", we *must* mean world.[10] For Austin, grammatical

8. Cavell's comments about dreams, I think, must be a reference to Michel Foucault's first published paper in which he uses Heidegger to show how dreams demonstrate not the zaniness of dream worlds, but the fragility of real worlds, how both are constituted. See Michel Foucault and Ludwig Binswanger, *Dream and Existenz*, ed. Keith Hoeller (Atlantic Highlands: Humanity, 1985).

9. J. L. Austin, "A Plea for Excuses," *Proceedings from the Aristotelian Society* 57 (1956–57) 1-30 (7). Regarding Austin's influence, see Stanley Cavell, *Little Did I Know: Excerpts from Memory* (Stanford: Stanford University Press, 2010) 277–78.

10. A comment in a graduate précis by Brandon Morgan started me thinking this way about "A Plea for Excuses." This point about excuses follows on Austin's initial argument where he puts forth an account of language that relates word and world as one of inexorable agreement, such as to pry them apart and theorize them back together as philosophical realists and anti-realists are wont to do is to ignore the ordinary conditions of human existence. We speak as we do because our life in the world bequeaths to us conceptual resources exactly for and even only for that life. As Stuart Hampshire explained in summarizing Austin: "For every distinction of word and idiom that we find in common speech, there is a reason to be found, if we look far enough, to explain why this distinction exists. The investigation will always show that the greatest possible number of distinctions have been obtained by the most economical linguistic means." Stuart Hampshire, "J. L. Austin 1911–1960," *Proceedings from the Aristotelian Society* 60 (1959–60) I–XIV (III). Cavell writes, "Too obviously, Austin *is* continuously concerned to draw distinctions, and the finer the merrier, just as he often explains and justifies what he is doing by praising the virtues of natural distinctions over homemade ones. . . . Part of the effort of any philosopher will consist in showing up differences, and one of Austin's most furious perceptions is of the slovenliness, the grotesque crudity and fatuousness, of the usual distinctions philosophers have traditionally thrown up. Consequently, one form his investigations take is that of repudiating the distinctions lying around philosophy—dispossessing them, as it were, by showing better ones. And better not merely because finer, but because more solid, having, so to speak, a greater natural weight; appearing normal, even inevitable, when the others are luridly arbitrary; useful where the others seem twisted; real where the others are academic; fruitful where the others stop cold" (Cavell, "Austin at Criticism" in *Must We Mean What We Say*) 97–114. Of course

investigations of things like excuses demonstrate how the ordinary work-ings of our life avail resources for that life. The problem with some philoso-phers is that, imagining language to do something other than make possible our life in the world, they make excuses for and then excuse away language, in favor of something better. The tragedy is that right before them, in front of their noses, as Wittgenstein says, failing to be impressed by that which is most impressive, are the very things we have deemed necessary for living.[11]

Because specific words are used for specific things and not others, because we know to do this and not that when this versus that happens, because we must mean what we say because what we say has been given meaning before our saying it, then constraint makes possible meaning and so our wording of the world and our mutual attunement in it. However while these constraints entail some things, they by necessity constrain other

---

our words are sufficient for our life in the world, otherwise they would not be our words; if they did not serve our needs, we, desirous creatures that we are, would not use them. Our language bespeaks the discursive history of our desires. Language is natural to life in the world in just this way. Excuses, for Austin, serve as an exemplary case of language qua language—in this case, a device we have found useful, stemming from the peculiar features of humanness, for going on in the world, especially since by "going on" we mean "going on together." It is not by coincidence that we have excuses; we are excuse-needy people, and if you are not, you live with them; our bodies fate us to excuses. Another such device so evolved over time might be apology as a way to go on when excuses run out. Austin's first point is that for every thing in our language there is a reason; over time that to which our interests drew us, we found ways of speaking about and those things we lost interest in fell by the wayside. (For another example, see Julius Kovesi's marvel-ous account of "misticket" in *Moral Notions* (London: Routledge & Kegan Paul, 1967) 46–53.) This, what Austin calls "the natural economy of language", also means that we should not use words but for the ordinary things they are meant to do—hence Austin's ascetic procedures of empirical investigation—and if we do so without good reason, we will surely pay a price. One might think of analytic philosophy's scholasticism as such a price. Sandra Laugier refers to the "analytic scholasticism" that has determined the course of philosophy since Quine. See Sandra Laugier, *Why We Need Ordinary Language Philosophy* (Chicago: University of Chicago, 2013). To get a sense of this price, imagine a world in which you were prohibited the use of excuses even though the prescriptive language-games of "being on time" or "in sickness and in health" continued; none could ever be caught needing an excuse, and so how would one live? Or imagine a world where excuses did bear meaning but forgiveness did not; one could never be caught without an excuse. Everything is there before us in our words; our life in the world requires that be the case. This is what Cavell means when, following Austin, he says it is we who are responsible for the maintenance of our language.

11. Ludwig Wittgenstein, *Philosophical Investigations*, trans. G. E. M. Anscombe, P. M. S. Hacker, and Joachim Schulte (Oxford: Wiley-Blackwell, 2009) §129.

things.[12] That our language is enabled by constraint and entailment means that if you use words for purposes unrecognized or unaccepted, or if you don't know what to do when someone says or does this, or you hear this as that and not this, or if you don't mean what we mean when you say what it is you say, well, then you are in trouble.

"The world is our word," Fleming says, by which he means the world is held together by linguistic constraints and entailments populating the natural conventions of the human form of life.[13] This also means that some will not fit with us, that a world of constraints and entailments will rule some out, leaving them on the outside looking in. We will not have words for them except those words that speculate what it must mean to be them, to be outside. In the excuses essay, Austin wrote, "however well-equipped our language, it can never be forearmed against all possible cases that may arise and call for description: fact is richer than diction."[14] We might call Anne Hauerwas a fact that is richer than diction, a reality that outpaces our ability to describe it. We can supply concepts that try to compensate for the lag between fact and diction, gestures like "the mentally ill" for a vast stretch of phenomena, but for their slippages someone will surely pay a price. Anne's life with Stanley is one such price, and she pays it alone.[15]

12. See Richard Fleming, *First Word Philosophy: Wittgenstein-Austin-Cavell Writings on Ordinary Language Philosophy* (Lewisburg: Bucknell University Press, 2004) 4. About this issue of relationship between constraint and suicide, Fleming writes, "The desire to be free of our past and not repeat it in the present, not be confined to an ongoing mad life controlled solely by others, can incite and force a dramatic choice, a choice between suicide and confession. These are acts of utmost personal freedom, since no one can commit suicide for you or confess for you. Another can murder you, drive you to your death, or speak for you, give you their words, but no individual, free expression accompanies such acts. Suicide and confession are ultimate expressions of individuality and freedom, unconditioned by others. They are existential, personal choices that destroy the repetition of the past and affirm either one's unity with the world (confession) or one's distance (suicide) from it" (*First Word Philosophy*, 67). I am indebted to K. C. Flynn for introducing me to Fleming's work.

13. Richard Fleming, *Evil and Silence* (Boulder: Paradigm, 2010) 4. Cavell distinguishes between "forms of life" in a horizontal conventional sense and in a vertical natural sense. See Stanley Cavell, *Philosophy the Day after Tomorrow* (Cambridge: Belknap, 2006) 207–8 as well as in the first part of *The Claim of Reason*.

14. Austin, "Plea for Excuses", 21. Our language comes to us equipped by the past for our needs. This says nothing about the future. The future of our words, as Stanley's good friend Peter Ochs explains, is "vague", as vague as the future itself. Peter Ochs, "Theosemiotics and Pragmatism," *Journal of Religion* 1 (1992) 59–81.

15. Sam Wells reminded me to note the diversity of issues "mental illness" attempts to cover.

(I did not say Stanley's life with Anne is that price, the cost there lies elsewhere and I will get to it.)

That we *can* mean what we say is language's most amazing trait; that we are not fated to do so is its most brutal trait, leaving some alienated from their words. These people come to mean by their words things they cannot possibly mean; they mean by their words things they should not mean. When they consistently fall short of "knowing what to do when" then it becomes apparent that they don't occupy the same world of meaning as we. And when they go on to insist that they do occupy the same world, and when this insistence continues, well then, we are all in trouble; things become very difficult. Fleming describes the difficulty.

> Recognition of the distance between saying and meaning (contemporary Western philosophy's mantra) creates confusion about whether we can, and how we can, mean anything. A loss of control of our words, which is an inevitable part of talk since our words leave us on their saying, threatens a loss of ourselves and madness. This is not a pleasant implication for the disciplined mind since the health of the human spirit is being entrusted to ordinary language controls, rather than to the transcendent truths or gods of a discipline or culture. It is far easier to embrace the intoxication brought by the latter than to face the sobriety of the former. Not knowing how to mean or say what we wish naturally numbs us, reintroduces silence, places the necessity of beginning again before us.[16]

About much of what Anne is given to saying in *Hannah's Child*, we think to ourselves, "She cannot mean what she says." She cannot mean what she says when she says she is in love with a celibate priest; she must not know what love or celibacy mean. And yet she does mean it. She cannot mean what she says when she says her deceased mother is using wallpaper

---

16. Richard Fleming, *First Word Philosophy*, 55. Fleming also writes, "It is this seemingly inevitable loss of control of our words that produces worry about being able meaningfully to express ourselves, generates a fear of inexpressiveness, and powerlessness to make myself known. Our failings at meaning what we say and others' questioning our meanings produce feelings of loss of connection *with the* world, loss of control over what our words say about the world and to others, and how others understand us and how we understand ourselves. Our loss of control is not necessarily over what words mean (we can fully know what words can mean, what words can be used to say or imply) but over what we mean in using them when and where we do, hence loss of the context of language use in which we speak, loss of meaningful expressions of myself and the world, hence the threat of madness and incoherence" (ibid., 28).

to communicate with her. But she does mean it. She cannot mean what she says when she says Adam cannot go and receive the sacrament. She means it. That she does is to us what is maddening about her; that we keep insisting to her that she does not is to her what I imagine is maddening about us.

Coming to terms with the human requirement that we mean what we say enables readers of *Hannah's Child* to appreciate Anne's difficulty, the price of her life with Stanley, as one of detachment from words, a detachment that must have left her with an awful longing for connection. No wonder she fell in love so often. How sad it must be to fall in love with someone who cannot share your world, someone who cannot make sense of your love, much less reciprocate it. Doubly sad that Anne could not, by the strictures of her illness, share any world with any person who could hold her to meaning what she said when she said she was in love. And so the sense of entrapment on the one hand and isolation on the other, descending into increasing and unending loneliness as detachment from words plays itself out in silence. Juxtapose this loneliness and silence with the friendship that Adam and his father shared, one so intimate that Professor Hauerwas worried it "might excommunicate Anne," and then the breadth and depth of friendships they had in the church. Erin Dufault-Hunter portrays the contrast vividly when she observes of him, "One of the things that strikes me about the difference from your life and Anne's is the excruciating loneliness of it. It's such a contrast to read about your life, and the fullness of your life with friends, that your life has been made possible, that you've been held, by friends."[17] In Stanley and Anne Hauerwas, we see played out before us what I called, reflecting on ordinary language, the amazing and brutal traits of our life in words: Stanley *doing* so much with words, Anne increasingly caught in the silence of detachment from words.

On several occasions, Stanley has confessed that he sought from Anne the words, "I know this is hard; thanks for sticking with it." Of course he would want that; any of us would. Inhabiting a common discursive world means, for Austin, knowing what to do when: *when* someone suffers with, for, and because of you, "I know this is hard; thanks for sticking with it" is not much but one can see how it could become everything. It is good and right to want that acknowledgment; those inhabiting the same moral space

17. "Reflections on God and Mental Illness." Or as Hauerwas himself said of Anne's isolation, "How lonely her life had been. That her loneliness was self-imposed does not make it any less sad. What possibly can be said about a life so lived. None of us should try to answer such questions. Our humanity demands that we ask them. But if we are wise we should then remain silent."

as we do know to say that or something like it. But this is precisely the kind of thing that Anne could not say, and her inability to do so exhibited the extent to which she had become alienated from our words. Stanley's unremitting desire to hear those words, the expectation that they occupied the same space (for how could they not?), must have been agonizing. That unanswered desire could not last, or at least it did not. Its end came with the recognition that Anne had gone off to a place from which she could not return, and to that Stanley finally relented, "I'm not coming." And so the price of Stanley's life with Anne.

One might object to my casting the difficulty of Anne as a difficulty of our common life in words by saying, "Yes, but isn't the difficulty really there, in her biochemistry?" Maybe, but the strangeness of Anne is not one of biochemistry, even if biochemistry may have something to do with her behavior. It is her behavior that is strange to us; "her biochemistry" but our attempt to account for that strangeness. To be sure psychotropic disorders like bipolar illness have their biochemical reasons, but those reasons do not get at what is so difficult about living with bi-polar illness. Our struggle is not with biochemistry but with persons whose biochemistries have been made to matter by what they say and do. Hence, Professor Hauerwas's rhetorical question as to what "mental" is doing in the locution "mental illness." We are tempted toward a concept of mind without bodies, and so imagine biochemistry, brain processes, and mental states as foundations of human being: "there it is, there is the source of the difficulty" in the "chemicals responsible for controlling the functions of the brain," the neurotransmitters like serotonin and dopamine.[18] And this ironic disembodiment goes further, locating the root of these issues in genetics and so of conditions that socially trigger bi-polar illness and its telltale episodes. Perhaps less bewitched would be *Hannah's Child* as a book of biochemistry. As Wittgenstein wrote in the *Investigations*, "Is it the body that feels pain?—How is it to be decided? How does it become clear that it is not the body?—Well, something like this: if someone has a pain in his hand, then the hand does not say so (unless it writes it), and one does not comfort the hand, but the sufferer: one looks into his eyes."[19] According to Cavell, in acknowledging pain we acknowledge persons in pain. According to Stanley, "it was the anger not the illness that finally exhausted me."

18. See http://www.nhs.uk/Conditions/Bipolar-disorder/Pages/Causes.aspx.

19. Wittgenstein, *Philosophical Investigations*, §286.

If one part of Professor McKenny's challenge is the question of whether exclusion from community is unavoidable. I'm afraid the answer is, "Yes, for the most part." McKenny's challenge read through Austin tells us that there are some things or persons or facts or aspects that a community's words simply cannot imagine. This in no way absolves communities of the responsibility that their languages require, including Christian communities for whom linguistic availability seems a natural entailment of inhabitation of the Word made flesh. It's only that the responsibility of one's words requires the maintenance of sense, ruling some uses out. Think here of how ascriptions some gave for Jesus—uses of words like "Emmanuel", "drunkard and glutton", "Messiah", "Beelzebul", "King of the Jews" —didn't quite work out. This doesn't mean that a community can never fashion the words, but just that it has not; maybe some other set of speakers will, just not the present one. Think here of how some ascriptions for Jesus—"Emmanuel", "Messiah", "King of the Jews"—have taken root. For Professor Hauerwas's theological ethics there is an important parallel, which we might call "being on the wrong side of a church's constraints and entailments." The cultural-linguistic appropriation of Wittgenstein that Hauerwas's "thick" account of church so powerfully advanced will, on the flip side, necessarily constrain what the church's speech can entail. Following John Howard Yoder, Professor Hauerwas believes that the politics of Jesus entails Christological pacifism. But that belief can't help but constrain certain Christian speech, detaching some from the very words they claim, leaving them with little to say that doesn't sound crazy within a church so thickened. For not a few Hauerwasians, I suspect, this is precisely the point, holding forth criteria that force some judgments out; it goes like this: "Given our liturgy, you can't possibly mean that!" To be sure, the outing goes both ways, but for us Christian pacifists, speaking well (without sounding patronizing) of brothers and sisters tied to the military becomes very tricky. And so for any number of issues in the church's "rush to community," as Peter Dula so aptly characterizes it.[20] While much of this comes with the territory—Christian community *is* thick with constraints and entailments—I imagine by "rush" Peter means to indicate that Hauerwasians have rarely taken stock of what thickness costs, but only what it gains.

---

20. Peter Dula, *Cavell, Companionship, and Christian Theology* (Oxford: Oxford University Press, 2011). Cavell remarks on the philosophical virtues and vices of "tolerance" in *Must We Mean What We Say?*, 96.

Part II: The Difficult Gift of the Church

I have tried to show that insofar as we are gathered through mutual attunement in language and insofar as Anne spoke in ways we could not make sense of, she remained beyond us. But this doesn't make her a surd. It just makes her human—that is, someone who shares in our human life in words; this is true even if her share issued without sense. This answers one part of McKenny's challenge. The other part is whether she is a surd to the particular story Stanley Hauerwas tells.

Let me restate the challenge in those terms then. Is Stanley self-deceived about the role Anne Hauerwas plays in his story? Is she, as McKenny put it, "the surd that resists your story, refusing to be assimilated into it and therefore reminding you of the limits of any account of Christian discipleship, including yours"? If the answer is Yes, if Anne is "an intractable argument against my theology," as Professor Hauerwas understood the challenge, then he is self-deceived insofar as he unwittingly set himself up for McKenny's conclusion: "My sense is she is [the surd that resists your story] and you did not really let her play that role." I take this question about self-deception—there is another to follow, about the church's ability to assimilate Anne—as a more personal version of the one often put to Professor Hauerwas regarding whether the church he heralds is actual, or mainly rhetorical, mythical, or tropic. In analytic terms, we can imagine someone without McKenny's subtlety of mind using Anne as a defeater case that proves Hauerwas's church theory invalid. As should be clear by now, I think Austin gives us reason to doubt both that argument and that *kind* of argument; if anything, I think Anne's role in the story makes for a richer-because-more-chastened account of the church triumphant. If we ever took Professor Hauerwas as trumpeting a church assimilating all difficulties to itself such that those difficulties end up less than difficult, we have misunderstood him. The church he speaks of is exceedingly difficult and unless we can receive it as such we will not have it as the gift he imagines it to be. I will turn to this in a minute.

Before doing so, I should say something about another kind of self-deception threatened by Anne Hauerwas. This would be the basic one where Professor Hauerwas narrates Anne in a way that deceives us about her history not because he has out-and-out lied but because he relates only his version of events. The concern here is that Anne Hauerwas is not able to read *Hannah's Child* and alert us to when she is being misrepresented. Because of Anne's death, there is no counter-narrative to *Hannah's Child*.

We might even say that because of Anne's illness, she could not provide anything approaching what we would recognize as a counter-narrative; it is all made to sound crazy. In those Fuller lectures on mental illness, it did not take long for someone to raise this very question. Precisely the question was: "We've heard a great deal over the period of three lectures about somebody none of us knows and the only narration we have is your narration, and I know through your writings that you are a morally sensitive theologian who would have seen from the beginning the ethical issue there, about narrating somebody's life who cannot speak for themself." Hauerwas responded,

> I knew I couldn't write about it until she was dead. I never talked about Anne much less wrote about her after she left, because of exactly the point you make. Because I am articulate, I had a power to articulate her life against which she was defenseless. There could be a violence in that that I certainly want to avoid. So I just didn't say anything . . . . I felt very much the problem you articulate, of not wanting to write about her in a way that didn't invite possible counter-narratives. . . . The only answer I can give [is that] I hope I have done an honest job of narrating her in a manner that doesn't make her the enemy.[21]

I think here we should simply acknowledge that Anne, whoever she was, including the possibility that she was not the person given to us in *Hannah's Child*, is not here, and so to judge whether her story was truthfully told is presently not within our powers. I think it is enough to say that *Hannah's Child*, as the title suggests, is Stanley Hauerwas's story, not that of Anne Hauerwas, and that Stanley could not tell Stanley Hauerwas's story without including his story about Anne. I also want to say that his telling his story as a story that has to include Anne makes for a story rich enough to at least name this temptation as a temptation. I will get to what I mean here by returning to the kind of self-deception I previously discussed.

Remember that I said that for Professor Hauerwas, the story that he tells of himself in *Hannah's Child* is a story of the church insofar as, by the end of the book, he finds the church has made him Christian. And so the story he tells of himself and the story he tells of the church are intertwined; the truthfulness of one bears on the truthfulness of the other, or at least it would seem to bear for the one who intertwines these stories. So as to the matter of whether Professor Hauerwas is self-deceived about the

21. "Reflections on God and Mental Illness."

church, and hence whether Anne proves an intractable argument against the church he has spent his career championing, is he self-deceived? My answer is this: The presence of Anne Hauerwas in his life tells us that the church Professor Hauerwas imagines Israel promising, Christ establishing, the Holy Spirit enabling, and God completing is a gift difficult to bear; at his best, Hauerwas has claimed this throughout his career.

Introducing *Truthfulness and Tragedy*, the book Nancey Murphy cleverly quoted when restating McKenny's challenge, Professor Hauerwas wrote, "My basic thesis here is contained in the title *Truthfulness and Tragedy*, for a truthful narrative is one that gives us the means to accept the tragic without succumbing to self-deceiving explanations."[22] Additionally, his famous essay with David Burrell on the Nazi Albert Speer states, "Self-deception is correlative with trying to exist in this life without a story sufficiently substantive and rich to sustain us in the unavoidable challenges that confront the self."[23] I see Stanley's life with Anne as the constant reminder that no matter how wonderful the church God in Christ established, it is, inasmuch as it is the sacramental presence of the crucified Christ, a gift almost impossible to bear. Though I would love to see the various brutalities recounted in *Hannah's Child* finally put to rest every accusation that Hauerwas is a sectarian fideist caught up in premature-eschatologically-inspired fantasies, I am a realist when it comes to the state of contemporary theology. But for me, I can't read *Hannah's Child* and not see that for Stanley "church" is a gift bearing the difficulty of reality.[24] Is Anne Hauerwas a difficulty *in* the story he wants to tell about the church? Undoubtedly. Is she a difficulty *for* that story? I'm not quite sure how to answer this question for it begs what one means by "that story."[25] If one understands Stanley's account of

22. Stanley Hauerwas, *Truthfulness and Tragedy: Further Investigations in Christian Ethics* (Notre Dame: University of Notre Dame Press, 1977) 12. "The task of theology is the integration of narrative and exploration. It is so because the quest to know and understand requires the activity we identify with the narrative of personal identity. Theology is done in the form of autobiography because it is the exploration of how the self can be written truthfully."

23. *The Hauerwas Reader*, ed. John Berkman and Michael Cartwright (Durham: Duke University Press, 2001) 207.

24. See Hauerwas's treatment of the "difficulty of reality" in Stanley Hauerwas, "Bearing Reality: A Christian Meditation," *Journal of the Society of Christian Ethics* 33:1 (2013) 3–20. Hauerwas in this essay makes use of Cora Diamond's "The Difficulty of Reality and the Difficulty of Philosophy," *Partial Answers: Journal of Literature and the History of Ideas* 1:2 (2003) 1–26.

25. I owe Erin Dufault-Hunter for making this point obvious. She writes, "Is she not

the church as one that can justify everything, well, then we would have to admit that Anne is a surd, but that admission would be about as dull as that story. But what if one imagined the story otherwise, not as destabilized by surds but as itself surd-like, a story that by the calculus of our entailments and constraints could not arrive but as random and unexplainable? What if the story is told in such a way that Anne becomes strangely consonant with the story's surd-like cadence, making Anne hardly stranger than that which Christ ordained through the vicar of the church: "When you grow old, you will stretch out your hands, and someone else will fasten a belt around you and take you where you do not wish to go" (John 21:18 NRSV). We can grant that Christian speech like all speech has its necessary entailments and constraints and we can grant that these entailments and constraints assign some to play the role of outsider, but *none of that* should be a problem for those who find themselves inside a story where random and unexplained events have been ordained as the norm. Ours is an adventure of irrational, unaccounted for, and even meaningless twists and turns which the Christian word "grace" is not meant to straighten out but to name. Of course knowing all this will not make life any easier, just like knowing something about biochemistry will not give us handles on the persons we live with. When knowing gives out and explanations reach bedrock, the skill that will benefit us is narrating the church in a manner that can hold together the church's entailed hope and the difficulty of its constraints; in an uncanny way Stanley Hauerwas is possessed of this skill, and more uncanny still is how his life has been made to display its manner.

As one way of developing what I have in mind here, let me read two different notes Stanley made related to Anne and Adam. The first comes from his earliest book, the 1974 *Vision and Virtue*. At the time he wrote, "My most important friends have been my wife, Anne, and my son, Adam. Together they have taught me most of what I have learned about what makes life worthwhile and joyful. They are gifts I cannot possess and are all the more valuable because of it. I thank God for them."[26] In a book that argues

---

a gift because she *is* a surd—but a gift Stan receives not only in seeking to live with her for so long but by allowing her presence in his story to challenge his own abilities for explanation? For those of us in the church who claim the gospel drama as our own plotline, Anne stands (again, as do all profoundly difficult conditions, experiences, and people of our lives stand) within and against the church's ironic tendency to neat platitudes" (Personal correspondence; included here with permission).

26. Stanley Hauerwas, *Vision and Virtue: Essays in Christian Ethical Reflection* (Notre Dame: University of Notre Dame Press, 1974) vii.

that the "goodness of persons is not automatic but must be acquired and cultivated," Stanley credits Anne and Adam as his most important teachers. At that time the severity of Anne's illness was still coming into view; this might have been one of those claims one makes before one knows what one is claiming. However, twelve years later, by the time ambiguity had given way to cruelty, in the 1986 *Suffering Presence*, Stanley writes in that preface, "As always I owe Anne and Adam everything, for they literally make my life possible. *They* suffer *my* presence day in and day out, not, I might add, without being a bit impatient with my considerable shortcomings but also always with love. With their presence I am gifted beyond measure."[27] It is significant that in that particular book, Stanley writes about pain, and what he writes about pain takes on a different light given what we now know about his life with Anne at the time of the writing.

When we are in pain we want to be helped. But it is exactly at this point that one of the strangest aspects of our being in pain occurs—namely, the impossibility of our experiencing one another's pain. It's not that we cannot communicate to another our pain. That we can do, but what cannot be done is for you to understand and/or experience my pain as mine. This puts us under a double burden because we have enough of a problem learning to know one another in the normal aspects of our lives; when we are in pain, our alienation from one another only increases. For no matter how sympathetic we may be to the other in pain, that very pain creates a history and experience that makes the other just that much more foreign to me. Our pains isolate us from one another as they create worlds that cut us off from one another.[28]

This experience of "stories we cannot share" Stanley calls "this quite common but all the more extraordinary aspect of our existence."[29] I view these words, words about unpossessable gifts and patient forbearance, as describing how Stanley has tried to understand the Christian conception of gift.[30] What we ought to notice is the proximity of gift to pain in these

27. Stanley Hauerwas, *Suffering Presence: Theological Reflections on Medicine, the Mentally Handicapped, and the Church* (Notre Dame: University of Notre Dame Press, 1986) x. Emphasis added.

28. Hauerwas, *Suffering Presence*, 76.

29. Ibid., 78.

30. I don't mean, by identifying Anne as "gift," to be sentimental, but only to indicate Hauerwas's freedom to identify her as gift. Hans Reindeers argues in Hauerwas and Wells's *The Blackwell Companion to Christian Ethics* that only those who live with the mentally handicapped can discover how it is they can be gifts. Doubtless, there are

accounts. Was Stanley unclear about the extent of Anne's illness in 1974? Probably. But in 1986 when he described Anne as a gift beyond measure, was he self-deceived about what was going on with Anne? I doubt it. Rather, he is claiming that gift, for Christians, is structured in a very particular way, where gift remains ever proximate to pain.

In *Truthfulness and Tragedy*, Stanley names a persistent temptation for Christian ethical reflection—the "attempt to let us have our moral commitments without willing the tragedies that they necessarily involve"—and what I want to conclude is that the goodness of Stanley Hauerwas's theology is that it teaches us *how* to wait for God and God's surd-like coming.[31] I stop short of using the word "tragedy" here as Stanley did there, because while I can see how "tragedy" registers something important, I fear referring to things as tragic obscures something about the kinds of creatures we are, as I have tried to intimate by my brief excurses on ordinary language. I don't want to say Anne Hauerwas was a tragic part of Stanley Hauerwas's story; I want to say she just was, is, and remains part of that story, that the story of Stanley Hauerwas can't be told without entailing something about Anne Hauerwas. The difficulty of Anne Hauerwas, it seems to me, is not that she cannot be so easily integrated into the story Stanley wants to tell; rather the difficulty is that the story he wants to tell will always entail such difficulties; the church of Stanley Hauerwas necessarily involves Anne Hauerwas; it is constrained in just this way, it entails these kinds of features. The entailment of such difficulties constrains what can be presumed about the church's ability to render difficulties less difficult. And yet the church is called to do just that, render some difficulties less difficult; it is just that the church in time does not know which of the difficulties she is called to carry will be made less burdensome and which will not; all she knows is that she is to carry the burdens given to her. She has to presume that the Holy Spirit is making all things new and so swords are made into plowshares and leopards lie down with the kid. But that doesn't mean everything will be made new in this time, every weapon made to feed, that every kid will survive. But it might, and this "might" has been enabled. Right up to the end, Anne Hauerwas *might* have been made well. And this was part of the difficulty, and hence why it was right for Stanley to want those words, and

---

plenty of differences between the mentally handicapped and mentally ill, but none that would detract from using Reinders here. Hans S. Reinders, "Being Thankful: Parenting the Mentally Disabled," in *The Blackwell Companion to Christian Ethics*, edited by Stanley Hauerwas and Samuel Wells (Oxford: Wiley-Blackwell, 2004) 427–40.

31. Hauerwas, *Truthfulness and Tragedy*, 69.

so agonizing when they did not come. Or it might be that everything is presently being made new yet in ways not readily apparent to us. Part of the gift of Anne Hauerwas and so many difficulties we discover along the way is how these gifts ground every aspiration the church might have for itself, demonstrating that Christian discipleship includes at least two things: the work of redemption and the work of redemption when redemption comes slowly.

On this point, I cannot help thinking that Anne Hauerwas has been, rather than a defeater to Stanley's theology, the subtext that fashions its most subtle contours. Think for a minute who else occupies his stories: uncle Charlie, Martha, Pipken, his young friend "Bob", Mrs. Proudie, Ian Bedloe, Job and his friends, Israel, the apostle Paul, and Jesus of Nazareth. Or recall those masterful Hauerwas one-liners: "Christian discipleship is extended training in how to die well and early"; "martyrdom is the church's most determinative form of witness"; "raising your children Christian means raising them to suffer"; "the courageous have fears that cowards never know"; "what do you mean *we*, white man?"; Hauerwas's rule: "you always marry the wrong person," and even more daunting, "you always marry the right person." Consider the arguments: that modern medicine is premised on the lie that we can get out of this life alive; that liberalism's reliance on the state is an indictment of the church's failure to be the church; that consequentialist and deontological normativity is what you do when you lack character, and if you've come to seminary to find that character, it's too late for you; that "Christ's life and crucifixion are necessary to purge us of false notions about what kind of kingdom Jesus brings." These are difficult matters, difficult demands. While it is true that we moderns live by the presumption that you should have no story other than the story you chose when you had no story, living the church's story, to use one of Stanley's favorite metaphors, is no bowl of cherries either. I worry that too often Stanley has been read, by Hauerwasians and anti-Hauerwasians alike, as suggesting a triumphalist narrative to which Anne Hauerwas can only be a surd in that dull sense, a "defeater" in the philosophical parlor games we are wont to play. Whereas it seems to me that the story to which Stanley keeps pointing us over against our proclivities to make it dull is the story of the church and its promise and wonder and what that promise and wonder necessarily entail and constrain in the very logic of its grammar. If the Anne Hauerwases of the world were defeaters on the storied salvation we call church, well then, indeed it would be dull. Anne Hauerwas is a difficulty of that story, a difficulty of the church, and in this way, the church of Stanley Hauerwas is a difficult gift, and only as such is it a gift. It was an incompletion to ever hear Stanley's story without hearing the role Anne played in it, just as it's been a mistake to receive Stanley's church without its attending and necessary difficulties; this is the condition of our stories, the very possibility of any triumph we Christians dare claim. If we have asserted Christian unity over against non-Christian division, the coherence of our liturgy over against liberalism's incoherence, or the church's peace over against the world's violence, if we have proclaimed any of these without also at least intending the difficult conditions under which that coherence, liturgy, and peace come about, the inestimable constraints and entailments, then we have yet to understand that the church's coherence, liturgy, and peace come as a sword, that the terms of the Kingdom's coming are nothing less than the end of this present age. When we invoke the Eucharist in a triumphalist tone we seem to have forgotten in what way it can play a critical role in theological ethics—the Eucharist means that the incarnate God died. If for us the presence of a difficulty so difficult that someone had to die makes the church's story less enticing, well then, we have missed something about that story and there-fore the conditions of the resurrection it proclaims.

I have an admission to make, and maybe at the end of this talk is the only place I can make it. Prior to seminary here at Duke, I had never read a Hauerwas book. I came here for the basketball. Which is ironic because while I attended but a few games in my seven years at Duke, I am now an unabashed Hauerwasian. I today love the church Stanley speaks of almost as much as I love basketball, which sounds like a statement about my idola-tries, but it really is a profession of my love for the church. For me, and I think for so many of the students that came before and after me, I found in Stanley a powerful articulation of what the church had to be given what scripture said it was. Before ever reading it, I had the benefit of being intro-duced to a Christianity very similar to that which is offered in *The Blackwell Companion to Christian Ethics*, Stanley's "Big Book" written by his friends. And, what I love most about the great gift of calling Stanley Hauerwas a friend and teacher, and what I imagine is most lovable about Stanley Hau-erwas for many of us here today, is his willingness to, invoking one of those titles again, name the silences, requiring that our sky-high theologies sit with the difficulties, to not allow academic pretense or a fluffy pietism or neat narratives to belie the fact that we Christians hold this promise but in earthen vessels. I came to Stanley with not a lot of Hauerwas, and certainly with not very much preparation, but I did come carrying my own difficulties, and I sensed in him a vision of church where questions often found inspiring answers and when not, the church as a place patient enough to let questions lie, a place able to abide difficult gifts, gifts as difficult and as good as Anne Hauerwas, Jonathan Tran, and yes, Stanley Hauerwas.[32]

32. I am indebted to Carrie Tran, Erin Dufault-Hunter, K. C. Flynn, John Wright, Natalie Carnes, Sam Wells, Matthew Whelan, and Ralph Wood for commenting on earlier drafts of this paper.

The Limits of Theology:
A Response to Jonathan Tran

Peter Dula

ALLOW ME TO START with a story. It is a story many of you have heard before, and while usually I recognize that it can be a bit tedious to recite over and over again one's best stories, on this occasion, in honor of one who is a master of shamelessly repeating his stories, it seems appropriate. I came to Duke in the spring of 1998 for the weekend when students admitted for the next year all come to campus. On one of those nights there was a party at the home Chris and Rachel Huebner shared with Amy and Peter Frykholm. I was in the kitchen with Stanley, and he was helping me sort out whether to come to Duke or to go to another school where I had been accepted. He said, "Well, if you go there, so and so will turn you into a good liberal ironist." I was young and dumb and thought *Contingency, Irony and Solidarity* was one of the best books I had ever read, but I wasn't so dumb as to ask "What's the matter with that?" So instead I asked, "And if I come here, what will you turn me into?" He looked me in the eye and growled, "A mean son of a bitch." Unfortunately for Jonathan, here I am . . . .

My remarks this morning are divided into three parts. In the first, I am going to make a comment or two about Jonathan's use of ordinary language philosophy. In the second, I raise some questions about Hauerwas's interpretation of McKenny's question, and in the third, I will try to say just why I think Jonathan's paper is a great one and specify what I think are the most important things for us to learn from it.

Ordinary Language Philosophy

My first concern, or set of concerns, about the first half of the paper, has to do with Jonathan's use of ordinary language philosophy. But let me preface them by saying that Jonathan's growing affection for that set of Wittgensteinians gathered around Stanley Cavell, and Hauerwas's turn, in some recent papers, to the same group, has been a source of great encouragement to me for which I am exceedingly grateful, not just because of fact that of the maybe a dozen copies of my book that sold to non-libraries, eleven of them were purchased by Baylor students.

Cavell, like Jonathan, is at pains to understand our separateness. He is as interested as Jonathan in "isolat[ing] or dramatiz[ing] the inevitable moment . . . of communication in which my power comes to an end in the face of the other's separateness from me."[1] But such descriptions are invariably in service of critiquing the ways philosophers attempt to justify or overcome that separateness—attempts to secure connections between insides and outsides, to have knowledge without acknowledgment, to turn metaphysical finitude into intellectual lack, all of which find ways to relieve us of responsibility for the other's separateness. Cavell writes, "There is no assignable end to the depth of us to which language reaches; that nevertheless there is no end to our separateness. We are endlessly separate, for *no* reason. But then we are answerable for everything that comes between us; if not for causing it then for continuing it; if not for denying it then for affirming it; if not for it then to it."[2] The first two sentences could be a summary of the first part of Jonathan's paper. But the last sentence sounds about as far as you can get from "If one part of Professor McKenny's challenge is the question of whether exclusion from community is unavoidable, I'm afraid the answer is, 'Yes, for the most part'" (61).

I have some misgivings about this conclusion. Ordinary language philosophy can be used to *describe* our separateness, but I am wary of using it to *justify* separateness. Here is Cavell again: "And if I say 'They are crazy' or 'incomprehensible' then that is not a fact but my fate for them. I have gone as far as my imagination, magnanimity, or anxiety will allow; or as my honor, or my standing cares and commitments, can accommodate."[3]

---

1. *The Claim of Reason: Wittgenstein, Morality, Skepticism and Tragedy* (New York: Oxford University Press, 1979) 122.

2. Ibid., 369.

3. Ibid., 118.

I don't doubt for a second that Jonathan knows this, but he is pushed in this direction, and can be excused for the direction, in part because the alternative seems to imply that Hauerwas is "answerable" for Anne's separateness. I seem to be using Cavell to judge Hauerwas's "imagination and magnanimity." That is not exactly false, but it is only obnoxious on a presumptuously narrow account of "answerability." More helpful would be to say that *Hannah's Child* shows us the forms Hauerwas's answerability took.

What McKenny Meant

But there is another reason that I think Jonathan is pushed in this direction and that is because at the beginning of his paper he takes for granted Hauerwas's interpretation of McKenny's question. McKenny had written,

> Is Anne one of the strange members of the Christian community whose presence with us teaches us how to be Christians, or is she the surd that resists your story, refusing to be assimilated into it and therefore reminding you of the limits of any account of Christian discipleship, including yours? My sense is that she is the latter and you did not really let her play that role.

Hauerwas takes McKenny to be suggesting "I may well not be aware of how profoundly Anne's life stands as an intractable argument against my theology." Jonathan glosses this as "Is there something about gathered communal life that necessarily excludes the possibility of full assimilation?" If those are the questions, then one might reasonably turn to philosophy to justify Anne's exclusion. But I think Hauerwas is misled here and in two ways. First, is it really about *Hauerwas's* theology? That reads too much into "including yours" and skips over "*any* account." She is a surd not just to communitarian theology, but also to ordinary language philosophy, to any theology or philosophy. And is it really an *argument*? A "reminder of limits" is only an argument if you have a very unHauerwasian understanding of theology. Maybe if you are John Milbank and you think theology is a slug fest in which you must outnarrate all competitors, a reminder of limits can only be an invitation to take the gloves off, but not if you think, as I learned to think here, that sometimes in theology you just have to muddle through.

I propose that the better way to understand McKenny's challenge is something like: "Tell this story in such a way that it acknowledges the fact that Anne doesn't fit. Tell it in a way that *lets* her play the role of a reminder of the limits of *any* account of Christian discipleship, including yours."

McKenny isn't saying that there is something wrong with Hauerwas's theology such that we can make a few revisions to it that would help him escape the force of the challenge to "any account." He isn't asking for a more elaborate account of Christian community and formation into which Anne could be made to fit *or* one that can explicitly justify why she doesn't have to. The former is impossible hence the latter unnecessary. But what would it mean to let the weight of that sink in? How would *Hannah's Child* and Hauerwas's theology *sound* different if Anne was allowed to be a reminder of limits, not a provocation to more argument?

Tran's Achievement

I think it would sound exactly like the second half of Jonathan's paper. I intend my rephrasing of McKenny's challenge as an account of what we just heard in the second half of the paper. Where the beginning of the paper takes for granted Hauerwas's reading of McKenny, the end does not. Jonathan's conclusion is this: "The difficulty of Anne Hauerwas . . . is not that she cannot be so easily integrated into the story Stanley wants to tell; rather the difficulty is that the story he wants to tell will always entail such difficulties" (8). Now, it seems to me, he is reading the challenge quite differently. He is no longer defending Hauerwas against McKenny but is performing on Hauerwas's behalf what McKenny asked. Jonathan is instructing us in how to read *Hannah's Child* in a way that allows Anne to be what, according to McKenny, Hauerwas didn't. In doing so, Jonathan has taught us something genuinely new about Hauerwas's theology, genuinely new, even if it was already there, waiting patiently for Jonathan to draw it out. At the heart of Jonathan's paper is this: "I cannot resist thinking that Anne Hauerwas has been rather than a defeater to Stanley's theology the subtext that fashions its most subtle contours" (68). That is now a challenge to all of us to go back and read Hauerwas with that in mind *and* to ask ourselves about the subtle contours of the theology each of us writes, to ensure that those contours are responses to pain, whether pain as personal as family and friends with mental illness, addictions, eating disorders, or as structural as the legacy of slavery or the fact of patriarchy.

Not only has Jonathan exposed something overlooked, it seems to me that he has enacted it. Notice how the very fact of Jonathan's paper attests to its central claim. The argument is that if you are going to journey with *this* church, the church articulated by Hauerwas, then you are committing yourself to confrontation with this kind of pain, refusing to avoid it but instead to bear it alongside others. That is what the paper said. But the evidence is not in the footnotes. The evidence is the simple fact of the paper. I confess I really did not want to talk about Anne Hauerwas this morning. I would very much have welcomed the opportunity to avoid that topic. I would like to avoid it for a number of reasons, many, perhaps all, of which make for the way, 'our pains isolate us from one another' to cite Tran citing Hauerwas. Pain doesn't isolate us all by itself. We make choices, or have choices made for us, about our pain that are isolating. Choices of avoidance, choices Jonathan has ruled out because, prompted by McKenny's question, he has discovered something about Hauerwas's church and is willing to publicly take the risk that, confronted with what he has discovered, we will react in recognition, not denial.

Third, it follows that there are consequences to failing to read Hauerwas properly. Most worrisome is the way Hauerwas "has been read, by Hauerwasians and anti-Hauerwasians alike, as suggesting a triumphalist narrative" (68). This is a concern that Jonathan, I suspect, has always been sensitive to, but in light of his reading of Anne, one that we are now all forced to take more seriously than perhaps we have. Jonathan writes, "*If* we have asserted Christian unity over against non-Christian division, the coherence of our liturgy over against liberalism's incoherence, or the church's peace over against the world's violence" (69) while downplaying the costs and difficulties, we misread something about this story. Now Jonathan knows very well that Stanley has asserted all these things and that we, his students, have also asserted them, some more than others and few less than Jonathan himself. Not as often and not in the ways, perhaps, that James Gustafson and Jeff Stout think we have, but we have done them. If we truly learn from Jonathan's paper, we will do so less often but that will make us more, not less Hauerwasian.

In closing, I want to say one quick word of gratitude to Stanley. Hauerwas likes to say that he had to become a pacifist because he is such a violent person. Or as he puts it near the end of *Hannah's Child*, "I have to tell people that I am committed to Christian nonviolence . . . because my life so belies that conviction. You do not have to be around me long to know that I am not exactly a peaceable guy."[4] The question of self-deception in this memoir was raised several times in Jonathan's presentation. Here I raise it not as a question but as an accusation. I know Hauerwas's public persona. And I

4. Hauerwas, *Hannah's Child*, 275.

haven't forgotten the times he has gotten, shall we say, frustrated with me for saying something too stupid or too liberal or both. But to claim that he is not a peaceable guy is a profoundly misleading account of the man who lived with Anne all those years, raised Adam, mourned Anne's departure, loves Paula with a love that should make a lot of wives very jealous, befriended so many academic colleagues (some of them rather questionable if you ask me) and others around the world, and taught, mentored, advised, counseled, even fathered, so many of us in this room.

4

Making Connections

By Way of a Response to Wells, Herdt, and Tran

Stanley Hauerwas

1. Context

"IN THE SHADOWS OF a dying Christendom the challenge is how to recover a strong theological voice without that voice betraying the appropriate fragility of all speech but particularly speech about God." I wrote that sentence some months ago. I am not sure what I was thinking about when the sentence occurred to me, but I suspect I was thinking about this event. I think I was trying to think about how I might characterize what I have tried to do over the years because I assume that is what you are supposed to do when you grow old or at least retire.

The sentence found me while I was working out. When I work out I often try to think about what I should think about given what I have thought about in the past. I do so in part in an effort to try to force myself to think thoughts that I should think given what I have thought. The latter task has resulted in a series of papers with titles such as "How I Think I Learned To Think Theologically," "How To Write a Theological Sentence," "How To Be Theologically Ironic," "How To (Not) Be a Political Theologian," "How To

Be Theologically Funny," "How To (Not) Retire Theologically," and "How to Be Caught By the Holy Spirit." I list the titles for you because I hope the titles suggest how I am trying to test and extend how I have tried to think in light of the sentence with which I began.

All of which is to say I hope to comment on these terrific papers by Wells, Herdt, and Tran by responding to them by way of the claim made by that sentence. So let me give it to you again: "In the shadows of a dying Christendom the challenge is how to recover a strong theological voice without that voice betraying the appropriate fragility of all speech but particularly speech about God." By so focusing my response to Wells, Herdt, and Tran I hope to show how their papers are interconnected and how that helps me understand some of the connections in my own work.

If what I have done has any lasting power I suspect it is through making connections between theological and philosophical commitments that often seem quite surprising because they have unanticipated implications. These connections are often quite loose but no less important, at least important for me, because I have to try to show why, for example, what I have learned from Wittgenstein has made a difference for the way I do theology. For I certainly hope Tran is right that the constraints and entailments that make our speech possible is true of what we say when we say "God."

I also think the connections I make between diverse philosophers, theologians, novelists, and activists are important. For example, in a "Foreword" I wrote for a new edition of Yoder's *The Priestly Kingdom*, I called attention to Yoder's claim that a "high Christology" is a "natural cultural ricochet of a missionary ecclesiology when it collides, as it must, with whatever cosmology governs the world it invades." I note that the connection between Christology and ecclesiology that Yoder's remark entails is the kind of move only someone well schooled by Troeltsch could make.[1] It was Troeltsch, the great Protestant liberal, who helped us see that how Christ is understood is determined by an ecclesial sociology. The relation of Christology and ecclesiology, as well as the relation of Yoder and Troeltsch, are the kinds of connections I hope are constructive for thinking through the practices that are necessary to sustain the church in a dying Christendom.

I must begin, however, by acknowledging that the sentence I am using to characterize my work suggests a far too coherent account of my work. In truth it is a sentence I have only been able to write recently, recent meaning

---

1. Stanley Hauerwas, "Foreword," to John Howard Yoder, *The Priestly Kingdom: Social Ethics as Gospel* (Notre Dame: University of Notre Dame Press, 2001) ix.

in the last twenty years, because I have never been able to give my work such a clear focus. Of course it may be that the sentence appropriately characterizes what I was doing early on, but if that is the case I did not know it at the time. I do think there have been continuities in my work from the beginning but those continuities and connections I often only discover later. I am not apologizing, because I think the most important moral judgments we make about our lives as well as how we think are retrospective.

I think both friends and critics of "my work"—and the very phrase "my work" always makes me nervous suggesting as it does possession rather than collaboration—often think that from the beginning I must have always known what I wanted or needed to say. In fact from the beginning until "right now," and by "right now" I mean this paper, I am usually just feeling my way through. For example, I had no idea that the moral psychology I was learning from Aristotle and Wittgenstein would entail a critical reaction to Rawls's account of liberalism. Herdt is certainly right that my account of the virtues might well be compatible with some forms of perfectionist liberalism, but I continue to wonder if even forms of perfectionist liberalism can give you the kind of politics necessary to produce agents who are not alienated from their action. As far as I am concerned, that is an open question.

Before engaging Wells, Herdt, and Tran, however, there is one aspect of my work to which I want to call attention because it generally goes unrecognized. I think what I am about to call attention to is important, however, because if it is ignored I think some of the connections I want to draw between these fine papers cannot be made. At the heart of my work, or at least at the heart of my heart, I have tried to give an account of what it means to be a Christian that does not avoid questions of truth. I am appropriately thought to be an ethicist or at least a theological ethicist, but I have tried to do "ethics" in a way that questions of truth cannot be avoided. That has entailed an ongoing exploration, as Tran's paper suggests, of how the language of the faith works to form lives.

Early on in my education I thought there was something right about the demand for verification of theological claims associated with the work of Anthony Flew and A. J. Ayer. Like many, I had trouble taking seriously their dismissal of theological and metaphysical commitments on the grounds they could not be verified by the verification principle, because that principle was itself not open to verification. Yet I thought there has to be something right, and by right I mean demanded by what makes us

Christian, about the need to show that to be a Christian entails a robust set of claims about the way things are.

Accordingly I was and have remained haunted, and I think that to be the right word, by John Wisdom's paper simply entitled, "Gods."[2] In his paper Wisdom asks us to imagine two people who return to their long neglected garden only to find that some of their old plants are doing quite well. One person concludes that while they were away a gardener must have been coming to tend the plants. But on investigation they can find no evidence that the proposed gardener has ever been seen working in the garden. The one that believes that there must be a gardener suggests the gardener must work at night. The other person says that cannot be true because someone sometime surely would have heard the gardener working—even at night.

The one who believes in the gardener, however, calls attention to the carefully arranged flowers to argue that someone who may be invisible must come to care for the garden. The believer thinks that if they just pay closer attention to the garden the necessary existence of such a gardener will be confirmed. They both study what happens to the garden when no attention is paid to it, but it turns out that no definitive conclusion can be drawn from empirical observation. Though they each see the same garden one accepts that a gardener must exist and the other does not.

What I like about Wisdom's parable is that it is not just a way to restate the verification principle. Indeed one of the reasons I have been attracted to the challenge the parable seems to present to those of us who believe that there is a gardener is the suggestion Wisdom makes about how such a believer might provide reasons for their conviction that a gardener exists. In particular Wisdom calls attention to the analogical reasoning associated with courts of law in which cases are compared. In such a context questions of fact are often settled but that is not the end of the matter. Rather a chain of reasoning can be developed to show why one party describes the situation as they do because of reasons they can give. It is the cumulative effect of such reasoning that makes the argument finally persuasive.

Wisdom calls this form of reasoning "the connecting technique."[3] He associates such a mode of reasoning with the kind of work necessary to reveal the beauty of a painting or to remove blindness we may have about

2. John Wisdom, "Gods" in *Logic and Language*, First Series (Oxford: Basil Blackwell, 1963) 187–206. Wisdom originally wrote the paper in 1946.

3. Ibid., 107.

some aspect of the world. Wisdom thinks this process, a process that is never ending, is the kind of reasoning that those who are convinced there is a gardener can use. To be sure the kind of connections required by those who believe in the gods is quite different than those who believe, for example, that flowers may feel pain. Yet both forms of belief entail what Wisdom describes as the management of language. For at the very least the development of reasons to sustain the belief that there is a gardener entails that the one making the connections be a certain kind of person.

As I suggested, I have always appreciated the way Wisdom shaped how questions about "gods" should be put because he avoided the cruder aspects of verification theories. Wittgenstein, not the logical positivist, was his philosophical teacher. I worry that Wisdom, the son of an Anglican priest, does not seem to have considered that in fact God is quite visible in Jesus Christ. Not only is Christ visible, but he has everything to do with the restoration of a garden. Of course the "visibility" of Christ can be seen only through the training Jesus demands of those who would be his disciples. I take such a point, however, to be one that is not inimical to Wisdom's parable. For whatever limits his parable may have, I nonetheless have found Wisdom's account an invitation to engage in an ongoing thought experiment that should keep our Christian feet to the fire.

It may seem odd for me to locate the kind of work I have done as a response to Wisdom's parable. Surely if you are to try to convince yourself or others that there is a gardener it would be better to begin with thin theological claims that do not ask you, for example, to believe that Jesus is the Son of God. Yet to assume as thin as possible a set of claims about God to try to convince someone else who does not share our faith in Jesus Christ I have always thought to be a mistake. It was the kind of mistake, moreover, that a church at home in the world would be tempted to make. Christians who are at home in the world are inclined to think everyone would believe what they believe if what they believed was explained in terms which every right-thinking person thinks. That is my way of describing the ideological role of Protestant liberal theology.

I have from time to time observed that I am a very simple believer. That confession is not meant to be a gesture of humility. Rather I assume I am a simple believer because what makes us Christian is not all that complicated. What we believe is fairly simple: God was in Christ reconciling the world through the work of the Holy Spirit. That is straightforward enough, but as is usual with straightforward claims they demand much thought. In particular they demand we be able to display the kind of community that must exist for the garden to be viewed as fruitful and beautiful. I hope that is what I have been about.

2. Wells, Herdt, and Tran

I should like to think the papers by Wells, Herdt, and Tran give evidence to support my claim that I have tried to do theology in a manner that refuses the distinction between theology proper and practical theology. Wells quite rightly begins by observing that the question for me has never been the difference I have made, but rather the question is the difference Christ makes. "Difference" of course can be a trap just to the extent an emphasis on difference can tempt you to emphasize distinctiveness as an end in itself. Yet I have sought to discover the differences because I think locating difference is crucial for questions about the truth of who we are because of what we believe. That does not mean that there is nothing in common between those who believe there is a gardener and those who do not, but too often what is thought to be "in common" does not do justice to the difference that agents make for what is thought to be common.

I am, after all, a historicist all the way down. There are many different forms of historicism, but if MacIntyre is a historicist then so am I.[4] If historicism, as Thomas Pfau suggests is the "dismantling of time into heterogeneous, incessantly 'lapsing' units of measurement correlates with the dissolution of the person into a series of states whose connectivity Locke is only prepared to accept as a hypothesis" then I am anything but

---

4. Robert Stern provides a very interesting account of MacIntyre's "historicism" in his "MacIntyre and Historicism," in *After MacIntyre: Critical Perspectives on the Work of Alasdair MacIntyre*, edited by John Horton and Susan Mendus (Notre Dame: University of Notre Dame Press, 1994) 146–60. He rightly calls attention to MacIntyre's claim that it is only when theories are located in history that demands for justification can be displayed without dogmatism or capitulation to skepticism. Stern calls attention to the history of art to display how progress is possible without assuming that some end point has been reached. In his "A Partial Response to my Critics" MacIntyre largely agrees with Stern's understanding of his historicism but argues that his historicism does not eliminate the notion of truth as does the kind of historicism associated with the Nietzschean tradition. See ibid., 297–98.

a historicist.[5] But I understand "historicism" to be the expression of the conviction that our lives as well as all that is can only be comprehended as narrative.[6]

My historicism is an expression of what I take to be the eschatological character of the Christian faith. Thus my conviction that church/world is a more determinative duality than nature/grace or creation/redemption. Put differently, my historicism is but an expression of the claim, "out of all the peoples of the world I have called you Israel to be my promised people." I, of course, believe that Jesus is very God and very man, but the doctrine of the Incarnation does not mean that any woman other than Mary could have been impregnated by the Holy Spirit. That is why I am so insistent that to believe that Jesus was the Christ, the second person of the Trinity, entails the relation of Jesus to the people of God, that is, the Jews.

If you are a historicist, it means that there is no place to begin because you can only begin in the middle even if you are unsure where the middle may be. That is but a way of saying you cannot escape the time and place in which you find yourself. My use of the description "dying Christendom" is an attempt to locate the time and place that must be taken into account for the work of theology today. I am well aware that description many may think very problematic, but like any significant description it begs for further display. In particular I have used that description to challenge the temptation to recover the power and status of American Protestantism by making the gospel subject to the desires shaped by the market. From my perspective, the only reason to be a Christian is that it makes you part of a people committed to telling one another the truth.

I have always presumed that such a people have no reason to think that we have nothing to learn from people who do not share our faith. So, of course, Christians will discover commonalities with those who are not Christian. What I have objected to is the assumption that what we may find we share in common can be insured by theory in a manner that removes

5. Thomas Pfau, *Minding the Modern: Human Agency, Intellectual Traditions, and Responsible Knowledge* (Notre Dame: University of Notre Dame Press, 2013) 37–38.

6. I have never been persuaded by Oliver O'Donovan's critique of historicism in *Resurrection and Moral Order: An Outline of Evangelical Ethics*, 2nd ed. (Grand Rapids: Eerdmans, 1994). O'Donovan argues that if everything is a story then there is nothing for the story to be about (60). Of course there is something for the story to be about; it just happens to be another story. I do not pretend that is an adequate response to O'Donovan's worries, but suffice it to say I have never been convinced by Strauss's account and critique of historicism. For an account of Strauss with which I have some sympathy, see Pfau, *Minding the Modern*, 51–52.

the necessity of actually getting to know those who are different. Common-alties may exist, but you will only discover that they do so by looking. I fear too often Christians have assumed an imperialistic position by declar-ing that they and their neighbors are essentially the same before they have looked. That strategy results in the separations so acutely named by Wells in his ten theses.

The ten theses Wells enumerates are not only an accurate account of what I think but, as is so often the case when I read Wells's account of what I think, I can only think, "I wish I had said that." But now I do not have to say it because Sam has said it for me. What I might be able to add to Sam's account is to suggest why the separations he so acutely identifies have been characteristic of modern Christian practice and theology. What happened that Jesus was separated from the church, or that Jesus's person and work were thought to be two things, or that Jesus as teacher could be distinguished from the crucified Jesus, or that the knowledge of Jesus could be known without the necessity of becoming his disciple? What made these "separations" make sense is, as I suggested above, is a correlative of the accommodation of the church to the world, which too often means Chris-tians try to have the results of the Gospel without Jesus.

So my claim that the first task of the church is to be the church so that the world might know itself as world is an expression of my fundamental Christological conviction that Jesus is who he says he is in the Gospels. Thus Sam's straightforward claim that the difference between church and world, simply put, is Jesus. That simple claim is why I can say in the "Intro-duction" to *War and the American Difference* that our task as Christians is not to work for the abolition of war, though that would be a "good thing," but rather our task is to be a people who live lives that are commensurate with our conviction that war has been abolished by the cross and resurrec-tion of Jesus.[7]

I do not pretend this claim that war has been abolished by Christ's cross is easily grasped. It is quite disorienting. It means, just as you should feel after reading *The Politics of Jesus*, that if it is true that war has been abol-ished by the cross you are not sure how to go on. I am quite sympathetic with those who do theology in a more conventional mode because even as one influenced by Barth and Yoder I find I still often revert to more accept-ed ways of doing theology. By more conventional ways of doing theology,

7. Stanley Hauerwas, *War and the American Difference: Theological Reflections on Violence and National Identity* (Grand Rapids: Baker, 2011) ix–x.

I mean how both liberal and conservative theologians often think you can get your doctrine of God straight without thinking about war.

For example, I think the attempt to characterize salvation in terms of satisfaction accounts of the atonement presumes that the Gospel is not a politics. In an effort to be politically relevant, Christians accepted the presumption that "real politics" is "out there" and thus were no longer able to make sense of the politics of Jesus. But you still have to say something about salvation because salvation language is all over the New Testament. Under such a regime salvation becomes associated with the relation of the individual to God, which the church may mediate but is itself not constitutive of. Doctrines of atonement seem necessary once the church is no longer seen as a people who can challenge the powers.

Jennifer and Sam call attention to how I have narrated the development of Christian ethics in America. That history I fear confirms what happens when the politics of Jesus has been lost. As a result, Christological convictions that make the distinction between church and world intelligible are simply not doing any work once the subject of Christian ethics in America becomes America. The political reality of the church is occluded by the overriding desire, in the words of Richard Rorty, to achieve our country.[8] With great charity Jennifer suggests I am not nearly as negative about the world as my rhetoric may sometimes suggest. She quite rightly, moreover, calls attention to my understanding of how the church/world distinction runs through each of our bodies. This is certainly true, but it is important to remember that the best picture of the soul we have is our bodies.

I am very sympathetic with Jennifer's admonition that truthfulness must be nourished not only by our being prepared to listen not just to our weakest members but also to those who regard themselves as quite foreign to the body of Christ. I am sympathetic with that admonition because I often think the person I know that most nearly fits the description of being an alien in the body of Christ is me. I have sometimes worried that my emphasis that it is time for Christians to take themselves seriously as Christians is overcompensation for my general sense that I may at best only be half-Christian.

---

8. Richard Rorty, *Achieving Our Country: Leftist Thought in Twentieth-Century America* (Cambridge: Harvard University Press, 1998). I use Rorty's way of naming the kind of piecemeal reform of economic injustice he thinks the left should be about because it is so close to the way Reinhold Niebuhr taught us to think. The only difference, of course, is Rorty sees no reason to think we need Niebuhr's Christianity to sustain the endeavor.

I worry I have been a master of Malesic's strategy of secrecy just to the extent that I do not even know how I may have been less than I should want to be. But I think Jennifer is certainly right, and I have responded to Malesic in a similar way—to wonder how secrecy can provide an effective response to the dangers of rationalization and self-deception. Bonhoeffer's understanding of secrecy was a Christological claim that reflected what he had learned from the monks about the communal power of silence. It was not a political strategy.

I suspect silence is the more appropriate stance for Christians than secrecy if we are to avoid the triumphalism that worries Malesic.[9] The refusal of Jesus to respond to Pilate is surely the crucial exemplification of the stance we must sometimes assume as witnesses to the Lordship of Christ. Such silence should express our commitment to nonviolence and our regard for the dignity of our adversary.

I thought it would have been interesting if Jennifer had developed her discussion of secrecy by reminding us of her account of those she calls "the Anatomists" in *Putting on Virtue: The Legacy of the Splendid Vices*.[10] Her discussion of Gracian's and Pascal's struggle to provide an account of virtue in social orders dominated by manners—that is, social orders that make it difficult to distinguish people of character from those who only appear virtuous—I think is must reading for anyone in the world in which we find ourselves. I confess from having read her chapter I have become a great fan of Gracian's wisdom about how one can and should cultivate appearances and the regard of others without ever appearing to do so. Advice I assume is relevant to this occasion.[11]

9. For a fascinating account of the history of the church as a history of silence, see Diarmaid MacCulloch, *Silence: A Christian History* (New York: Viking, 2013). MacCulloch makes the important point that silence can be used to avoid the recognition of the sinfulness of the church.

10. Jennifer Herdt, *Putting on Virtue: The Legacy of the Splendid Vices* (Chicago: University of Chicago Press, 2008) 221–47.

11. I am thinking in particular of Gracian's advice not to flaunt your good fortune. He observes: "It is more offensive to take excessive pride in your high office than in yourself. Don't play the 'great man'—it is odious—and don't be proud of being envied. The more strenuously you seek the esteem from others, the less of it you will have. It depends on respect. You can't simply grab it, you have to deserve it and wait for it. Important occupations call for a certain gravity and decorum. Keep only what the occupation requires, what you need to fulfill your obligations. Don's squeeze it dry; help it along. Those you want to look like hard workers give the impression that they aren't up to their jobs. If you want to succeed, do so using your gifts, not your outer trappings. Even a king ought to be venerated more because of his person than because of his pomp and circumstance."

But then I am not sure there is any way that I can provide an effective response to our endemic temptation to self-deception. I am sure there is no way to avoid self-deception if we think we can do it on our own. Indeed I know of no way to avoid self-deception other than to have friends, who from time to time may seem more like enemies, who will tell us the truth. There simply is no alternative to self-deception if there does not exist communities shaped by habits of truthful speech.[12]

That is why I think the best response I have to Jennifer is Tran's paper. It is a courageous paper because Tran knows what he has done risks being misunderstood. This is the academy. This is where we learn to have disagreements without taking it personally. But Tran's account of Anne is intensely personal. Of course that what Tran has done is intensely personal is appropriate because I did in fact write a very personal book called *Hannah's Child*. As usual I am not sure what led me to write *Hannah's Child*, but I found myself saying when asked why I wrote the book that I wanted to remind people I am a human being.

I am aware that response may seem arrogant. Of course I am a human being. What else could I be? But that response is but a commentary on the sentence "I did not intend to be Stanley Hauerwas." That sentence was my attempt to distance myself from that creature who is allegedly famous, while taking some responsibility for others taking seriously what I have said. It is a sobering thing to be told by someone you have made a difference in their lives. Some have even told me that what I have said or written has made it possible for them to be a Christian. Such declarations are at once gratifying and frightening given my own sense of what an inadequate witness I know myself to be. I can say, as I have said, that theologians should never let the limits of our lives determine what we should say as servants of the church. Yet I cannot help but be chastened when observing that others live what I say more faithfully than I am able to live.

Tran directs attention to Richard Fleming's observation that it is no easy thing to "attempt to find ourselves in the complexity of the systematic

---

The Art of Worldly Wisdom, translated by Christopher Maurer. (New York: Doubleday, 1992) 58–59.

12. Gracian works hard at avoiding self-deception observing: "Don't lie, but don't tell the whole truth. Nothing requires more skill than the truth, which is like a letting of blood from the heart. It takes skill both to speak it and to withhold it. A single lie can destroy your reputation for honesty. The man deceived seems faulty, and the deceiver seems false, which is worse. Not all truths can be spoken: some should be silenced for your own sake, others for the sake of someone else." Ibid., 102.

order of our words, the words we share." We are, according to Fleming, never free of failing to mean what we say. Thus the necessity of saying, "What I really meant to say was X and not Y." We use words that are not our words which mean we cannot help but lose control over what we mean when we use them. Thought requires, therefore, that we must struggle "to mean what we say using words that are not our own. We find we are fated in the language of our ancestors, in the language we inherit from them. Hence to understand what words mean we must understand what those who use them mean."[13] But we must also remember that those to whom we look for understanding what we say or have said may not have understood what they have said.

Niklas Forsberg, in a recent book on Iris Murdoch, explores Murdoch's contention that we are living in a time in which we have "suffered the general loss of concepts."[14] Forsberg argues that when we lose the sense of our words, when our words are worn and torn, we can miss the fact that the words we use no longer do the work they once did even though we continue to use those words. These are extremely complex matters involving questions of the relation of words to concepts, but I call attention to Forsberg's account because what I have tried to do is to help us locate the kind of lives necessary to make sense of the way we should speak as Christians.[15]

13. I am currently reading Jean-Luc Marion's, *In the Self's Place: The Approach of Saint Augustine* (Stanford: Stanford University Press, 2012). Marion's account of Augustine's understanding of the place of the self could I think be fruitfully compared with Tran's use of Fleming. Marion argues that our misunderstandings of Augustine are due to our attempt to read him within our metaphysical conditions of thought. The task, according to Marion, is "to approach the side from which Saint Augustine thinks to find there what he tries to think: the itinerary of an approach to the place of self—to the place of the self, the place most foreign to he who, proximally and for the most part, I am, or believe myself to be" (xiv).

14. Niklas Forsberg, *Language Lost and Found: On Iris Murdoch and the Limits of Philosophical Discourse* (New York: Bloomsbury, 2013) 2. Murdoch's claim is from her essay "Against Dryness," in *Existentialists and Mystics*, edited by Peter Conradi (New York: Penguin, 1999) 290.

15. Forsberg calls attention to Cora Diamond's suggestion that "Murdoch is not saying, as MacIntyre is, that we lack the kind of life within which such concepts as we need could be intelligently applied. He says we are naked irrational wills disguised as moral reasoners; she . . . says that what goes with our present depleted moral vocabulary is that we appear to be such wills." *Language Lost and Found*, 214. To the extent one can be clear about the difference between MacIntyre and Murdoch on this matter, I suspect I am closer to MacIntyre's view.

Miss Murdoch thought the novel was the appropriate form to recover the concepts necessary to recognize how to live as contingent beings. I do not have Murdoch's talent, but I do have a story called "gospel" that I believe has the language necessary to make possible the acknowledgement of our contingency in a way that gives us the ability to go on. An ability that Murdoch I suspect did not think possible. The shorthand name for that story is called "hope."

Tran suggests that the difficulty of saying what we mean is intensely embodied in my life with Anne. It is not clear we have ever had sufficient concepts to know how to understand what we mean by mental illness or how to care for those suffering from that condition. That Anne was an unavoidable presence, a presence that defied explanation, in my life Tran thinks makes doubtful any idea that I think what it means to be a Christian or the church means we can exist without difficulty. I hope he is right about that. But that recognition requires the recovery of Christian speech, for without the grammar of that speech, a grammar as Wells rightly maintains is determined by the crucifixion, self-deception will always be waiting in the wings.

Let me give you one more time the sentence with which I began: "In the shadows of a dying Christendom the challenge is how to recover a strong theological voice without that voice betraying the appropriate fragility of all speech but particularly speech about God." Wells is the strong theological voice that makes possible the language we need to sustain the church that Jennifer quite rightly says must listen as well as serve the world in a manner that as Christians we never pretend, as Tran argues, to know more than we do. Which means I must try to say more truthfully than I have some things about my life by commenting on one aspect of Tran's paper.

In particular, I want to comment on the sentences to which he calls attention in the "Preface" to *Vision and Virtue* and *Suffering Presence*. *Vision and Virtue* was published in 1974. At that time Anne was troubled but she had not yet had a dramatic psychotic break. I suggested in that "Preface" that she and Adam were gifts that taught me what makes life worthwhile and joyful. In the "Preface" to *Suffering Presence*, a book published in 1986, which meant the Anne's life and Adam's and my life were now dominated by her illness, I expressed my debt to Anne and Adam suggesting they suffered my presence with love.

I remember early in our relationship Paula read those prefaces and asked if they were true. They were certainly true about Adam, to whom I later dedicated *Christian Existence Today*, observing that in spite of what Aristotle says about how unlikely friendship is between fathers and son we are deep friends. But the claim in the earlier books that Anne made life joyful and suffered my presence with love was not true. What was true about those sentences was how in the unlikely chance Anne might read them they were my desperate attempt to have her take some ownership of our lives. Those sentences were hopeless gestures of hope.

I call attention to Jonathan's quite perceptive account of what I said in those prefaces because I need to say I am simply not sure how Anne's life made a difference for how I think. When I wrote *Truthfulness and Tragedy* several friends who were aware of Anne's illness thought "tragedy" must be my way of trying to understand what we were going through. That was not how I thought about our circumstance. I thought our situation was filled with pathos but not tragedy. In fact I remember trying very hard not to let Anne determine what I thought I should say as a theologian. I have no idea how successful I was in that endeavor.

We are such subtle creatures. I report in *Hannah's Child* that friends would often commend me for sticking it out for so many miserable years. I never thought I deserved any recognition for doing what I was doing. In fact I remember worrying if I finally walked out whether I could sustain the kind of edge I thought I needed to do the theological work I was doing. So I was "using" Anne to insure I would not become just another academic theologian. We are such subtle creatures.

But that is not how I survived. I survived through the significance of friendship. The first and most important friendship was with Adam, but I was fortunate to have many friends claim me as a friend. I have often observed it is one thing to be lonely by oneself. It is quite another thing to be lonely with someone. I experienced the later form of loneliness, a loneliness I suspect is more common than we acknowledge, though perhaps not in the intense form that was characteristic of my life for many years. Friendship saved me.

And humor. I could not have survived without humor. Jonathan is quite right to emphasize the difficulty being Christian and the church entails, but the other side of difficulty is a profound joy that makes possible the living through the difficulties with the confidence that God is in all this. I think, moreover, that often what is missing by the church that fears the world is a profound lack of a sense of humor. For it surely must be the case that the presumption that the church is the people of God, a presumption I think is true, means often that the joke is on us. After all when everything is said and done all this is about God and God's desire to have us as friends. That has got to make you happy.

That does not mean that there is no place for anger. I can be quite angry, but I do not think being angry is incompatible with being happy. I cannot pretend, however, that my anger has been directed at forces Sam identifies as injustice, privilege, elites, and oppression.[16] Of course I am against injustice, but locating injustice as well as knowing what to do about it is no easy thing. In so far as anger has shaped my life, my anger has been directed more toward the church (and myself) for failing to acknowledge and respond to the powers that insure that so many must lead such miserable lives.

I strongly believe in the diversity of gifts in the Christian community. No one of us can do everything that needs to be done. Others are better at social policy and strategies to challenge injustice than I am. I just want them, as Sam suggests, to remember, as the Syrophenician women remembered, the difference Jesus makes—a difference I should like to think I have identified rightly in the work of Jean Vanier. For it is surely the case that his way of helping us see the significance of the refusal to abandon a child that is born disabled is the kind of moral commitment that makes it possible to identify other forms of injustice.

I should like to think that any response to Wisdom's parable should begin with the work of L'Arche. That work, I am convinced, is unintelligible if the God we worship as Christians does not exist. It is, moreover, a work in time that believes we have been given all the time we need to be with those we unhappily label as the disabled. It is that work that makes concrete why the first task of the church is to be the church.

I am quite aware that my response to Wells, Herdt, and Tran is inadequate, but time is short and I must now say what needs to be said if I am to tell the truth about my life and work. In *Hannah's Child* I note that not everyone needs to become a theologian to be a Christian but I probably did. That is only half true. The truth is, I only became a theologian because I had

16. Nicholas Wolterstorff's recent book, *Journey Toward Justice: Personal Encounters in the Global South* (Grand Rapids: Baker, 2013) is an admirable account of how Wolterstorff was awakened by the suffering of others to pursue justice. Though I have some worries about how Wolterstorff understands justice, I appreciate deeply his candid account of how he was transformed by his encounters in the so-called third world. I use the word "awaken" in the sense developed by Oliver O'Donovan in *Self, World, and Time: Ethics as Theology* (Grand Rapids: Eerdmans, 2013) 9–17.

to recognize that I would never make it in the majors. I kept the hope alive until I was well into my 50s. It was only when my rotator cuff went bad that I realized my career even in church softball was over. Nevertheless, I cannot help but identify with the following speech.

3. "I am the Luckiest Man on the Face of the Earth."

"Today I consider myself the luckiest man on the face of the earth. I have been in ballparks for seventeen years and have never received anything but kindness and encouragement from you fans. Look at these grand men. Which of you wouldn't consider it the highlight of his career to associate with them for even a day." That, of course, is a portion of Lou Gehrig's great speech on his retirement from baseball because of his illness. He was suffering from ALS. Let it be noted that by calling attention to Gehrig I clearly demonstrate my willingness to learn from the stranger. Gehrig was a Yankee. We are talking American League here. All of which is testimony to how a genuinely great person can overcome the limits of their social location.

Yet it is true that I consider myself the luckiest person on the face of the earth. Look around you and you will understand why. Luck is a tricky notion for Christians, suggesting, and it may not necessarily be entailed by the concept of luck itself, that we are subjects of arbitrary fate. My life has been claimed by wonderful, extraordinary, often weird people in a manner that has made me more than I am. I could never hit a curve ball, but I have been surrounded by those who could. They made it possible for me to play the game.

In particular my life has been made possible by colleagues and graduate students who have persisted and sometimes been successful in their attempt to educate me. I think an interesting study could be made about how my colleagues and graduate students often forced me to read people whom I would have otherwise ignored. They have been my teachers, often teaching me what they were learning from other teachers in the university.

A reminder of how fortunate I have been to have a life spent in the university. Universities are, of course, envy machines, but that is just a way to indicate they are peopled by people. But what interesting people they are. To be with such people even for a day is a gift. The Yoders and the MacIntyres may not necessarily "get on" with one another, but they have been made friends in my life. Who would have ever thought that you could learn that much from a poet named Langland? How could you anticipate that someone named Foucault would help you see the cage called freedom? How could I have ever read with understanding, and some may dispute that claim, Augustine, Aquinas, and Newman without those with the patience of a scholar guiding me?

But I have been just as fortunate to have a life spent in the church. I am not sure we have the means to know in our time what Christianity looks like, but I know I have been surrounded by Christians who have made my life possible. To know that there is a day, let us call it Sunday, that makes a time possible for a people to be gathered to worship God, is a reality that should never be taken for granted. Indeed one of the gifts that I have discovered I cannot live without is the gift of time called worship. Broadway Christian Parrish, Aldersgate United Methodist Church, the Church of the Holy Family are names of people who have taught me to love God. God knows what the future of the church may be in social orders like ours, but I believe God is determined to make Christians interesting again. I hope I have had some small role in that project.

I have always been a person in a hurry. God knows why I have always been in a hurry, but that is why God is God and I am not. Persons in a hurry can easily miss the gifts that make the lives we have been given lives that can be lived. In particular we can miss God's reality in our lives because the Lord of time has no reason to hurry. One of the gifts I have been given to slow me down is called Paula. God is not present to me in the way God is present to Paula. I am not complaining but simply stating what I know to be true. Yet that she includes me in her love of God means all this "Christian stuff" is not just another game. It is not a game but rather a garden of endless delight.

And then there is Adam. He is a life that means Anne's life was not all darkness. Adam, now the son of Stanley and Paula, is a gentle and kind person in whom we delight and who delights us with his enthusiasm for life. Adam, Laura, Joel, and Kendall are names that signal what hope looks like. What miserable creatures we would be if we failed to recognize the gifts that make us human.

So my only wish on this day—a day that marks both an end and a beginning—is that what I have done over the years that have led to this day, as well as what I will do in the years to come, may in some way help us be what we were created to be, that is, creatures who rejoice in the salvation made possible through the gift of God's Son. "In the shadows of a dying Christendom the challenge is how to recover a strong theological voice without that voice betraying the appropriate fragility of all speech but particularly speech about God." We are fragile creatures who are masters at hiding our fragility. Fragility is but another name for contingency—we are utterly dependent creatures. We are the plants that need tending.

The strong voice needed in a dying Christendom will not come by shouting. The voice required to speak in this age and every age has already spoken. We simply have to learn to trust and inhabit that speech so that we may be called truthful; so that the world may see in us a truthful witness to the salvation of our Lord. You have been that witness for me. And I, in turn, have had the joy of bearing witness to your witness. I am truly the luckiest man on the face of the earth. What a wonderful thing it has been for me to serve such a people.

Service of Holy Eucharist
The Feast of All Saints
Goodson Chapel, Duke Divinity School

Friday, November 1, 2013
Seven Thirty in the Morning

PROCESSIONAL   *For All the Saints*   SINE NOMINE

1) For all the saints, who from their labors rest,   2) Thou wast their rock, their fortress, and their might:
   who thee by faith before the world confessed,   Thou, Lord, their Captain in the well-fought fight;
   thy Name, O Jesus, be for ever blessed.   Thou, in the darkness drear, the one true Light.
   Alleluia, alleluia!   Alleluia, alleluia!

OPENING ACCLAMATION
   Celebrant: Blessed be God: Father, Son, and Holy Spirit.
   People: **And blessed be his kingdom, now and for ever. Amen.**

* COLLECT FOR PURITY
   Celebrant: Almighty God, to you all hearts are open, all desires known,
   and from you no secrets are hid: Cleanse the thoughts of our hearts by
   the inspiration of your Holy Spirit, that we may perfectly love you, and
   worthily magnify your holy name; through Christ our Lord. **Amen.**

*GLORIA

> *All:* Glory to God in the highest,
> and peace to his people on earth.

> Lord God, heavenly King,
> almighty God and Father,
> we worship you, we give you thanks,
> we praise you for your glory.

> Lord Jesus Christ, only Son of the Father,
> Lord God, Lamb of God,
> you take away the sin of the world:
> have mercy on us;
> you are seated at the right hand of the Father:
> receive our prayer.

> For you alone are the Holy One,
> you alone are the Lord,
> you alone are the Most High,
> Jesus Christ,
> with the Holy Spirit,
> in the glory of God the Father. Amen.

> *Celebrant*: The Lord be with you.
> **People**:   And also with you.
> *Celebrant*: Let us pray.

*COLLECT OF THE DAY

Celebrant: Almighty God, you have knit together your elect in one communion and fellowship in the mystical body of your Son Christ our Lord: Give us grace so to follow your blessed saints in all virtuous and godly living, that we may come to those ineffable joys that you have prepared for those who truly love you; through Jesus Christ our Lord, who with you and the Holy Spirit lives and reigns, one God, in glory everlasting. **Amen.**

OLD TESTAMENT   *Daniel 7:1–3, 15–18*

PSALM *(responsively by whole verse)*   *Psalm 149*

1 Hallelujah!
  Sing to the LORD a new song;
  sing his praise in the congregation of the faithful.

2 Let Israel rejoice in his Maker;
  let the children of Zion be joyful in their King.

3 Let them praise his Name in the dance;
  let them sing praise to him with timbrel and harp.

4 For the LORD takes pleasure in his people
  and adorns the poor with victory.

5 Let the faithful rejoice in triumph;
  let them be joyful on their beds.

6 Let the praises of God be in their throat
  and a two-edged sword in their hand;

7 To wreak vengeance on the nations
  and punishment on the peoples;

8 To bind their kings in chains
  and their nobles with links of iron;

9 To inflict on them the judgment decreed;
  this is glory for all his faithful people.
  Hallelujah!

Celebrant: The Holy Gospel of our Lord Jesus Christ according to Luke.
***People*: Glory to you, Lord Christ.**

*GOSPEL   *Luke 6:20–31*

Celebrant: The Gospel of the Lord.
***People*: Praise to you, Lord Christ.**

SERMON   "All Saints"

THE NICENE CREED
Celebrant: We believe in one God,
**People: ....the Father, the Almighty, maker of heaven and earth, of all
that is, seen and unseen. We believe in one Lord, Jesus Christ, the
only Son of God, eternally begotten of the Father, God from God,
Light from Light, true God from true God, begotten, not made, of
one Being with the Father. Through him all things were made. For
us and for our salvation he came down from heaven: by the power
of the Holy Spirit he became incarnate from the Virgin Mary,
and was made man. For our sake he was crucified under Pontius
Pilate; he suffered death and was buried. On the third day he rose
again in accordance with the Scriptures; he ascended into heaven
and is seated at the right hand of the Father. He will come again in
glory to judge the living and the dead, and his kingdom will have
no end. We believe in the Holy Spirit, the Lord, the giver of life,
who proceeds from the Father and the Son. With the Father and
the Son he is worshiped and glorified. He has spoken through the
Prophets. We believe in one holy catholic and apostolic Church.
We acknowledge one baptism for the forgiveness of sins. We look
for the resurrection of the dead, and the life of the world to come.
Amen.**

*PRAYERS OF THE PEOPLE

CONFESSION OF SIN AND PARDON
Celebrant: Let us confess our sins against God and our neighbor.
People (kneeling or seated):
    Our heavenly Father, who by your love has made us, and through

your love has kept us, and in your love would make us perfect: We humbly confess that we have not loved you with all our heart and soul and mind and strength, and that we have not loved one another as Christ has loved us. Your life is within our souls, but our selfishness has hindered you. We have not lived by faith. We have resisted your Spirit. We have neglected your inspirations.

Forgive what we have been; help us to amend what we are; and in your Spirit direct what we shall be, that you may come into the full glory of your creation, in us and in all people; through Jesus Christ our Lord.

Celebrant: Almighty God, our heavenly Father, who of your great mercy has promised forgiveness of sins to all who with hearty repentance and true faith turn to you: Have mercy upon us; pardon and deliver us from all our sins; confirm and strengthen us in all goodness; and bring us to everlasting life; through Jesus Christ our Lord.

All: **Amen.**

*PEACE

Celebrant: The peace of the Lord be always with you.
People: **And also with you.**

*GREAT THANKSGIVING

Celebrant: The Lord be with you.
People: **And also with you.**
Celebrant: Lift up your hearts.
People: **We lift them to the Lord.**
Celebrant: Let us give thanks to the Lord our God.
People: **It is right to give him thanks and praise.**
Celebrant: Blessed are you, God of creation and of all beginnings . . . .
… we join in the song of unending praise, saying:

*SANCTUS

All: **Holy, Holy, Holy Lord, God of power and might,**

heaven and earth are full of your glory.

Hosanna in the highest.

Blessed is he who comes in the name of the Lord.

Hosanna in the highest.

Celebrant: Truly holy are you, and blessed is your Son Jesus Christ...
... Therefore we proclaim the mystery of faith:
All: **Christ has died. Christ is risen. Christ will come again.**

Celebrant: Send the power of your Holy Spirit upon these gifts . . .
... Through him, with him, in him, in the unity of the Holy Spirit, all
honor and glory is yours,
Almighty God, now and for ever.
All: **AMEN.**

*LORD'S PRAYER

**Our Father, who art in heaven, hallowed be thy Name, thy kingdom
come, thy will be done, on earth as it is in heaven. Give us this day our
daily bread. And forgive us our trespasses, as we forgive those who
trespass against us. And lead us not into temptation, but deliver us
from evil. For thine is the kingdom, and the power, and the glory, for
ever and ever. Amen.**

Celebrant: Alleluia. Christ our Passover is sacrificed for us;
People: **Therefore let us keep the feast. Alleluia.**

*SEQUENCE HYMN   The Disciples Knew the Lord Jesus   *MODE 6 MELODY*

Celebrant: The Gifts of God for the People of God.
Take them in remembrance that Christ died for you,
and feed on him in your hearts by faith, with thanksgiving.

DISTRIBUTION OF THE BLESSED SACRAMENT

The communion elements are bread and wine. Please wait to be directed to a communion station by an usher.

MUSIC DURING DISTRIBUTION   Let Us Break Bread Together   *LET US BREAK BREAD*

1) Let us break bread together on our knees (on our knees),
Let us break bread together on our knees (on our knees)
When I fall on my knees with my face to the rising sun,
O Lord, have mercy on me (on me).

2) Let us drink wine together on our knees (on our knees)
Let us drink wine together on our knees (on our knees)
When I fall on my knees with my face to the rising sun,
O Lord, have mercy on me (on me).

3) Let us praise God together on our knees (on our knees)
Let us praise God together on our knees (on our knees)
When I fall on my knees with my face to the rising sun,
O Lord, have mercy on me (on me).

4) Let us praise God together on our knees (on our knees)
Let us praise God together on our knees (on our knees)
When I fall on my knees with my face to the rising sun,
O Lord, have mercy on me (on me).

*POST-COMMUNION PRAYER *(in unison)*

God, the source of all holiness and giver of all good things: May we who have shared at this table as strangers and pilgrims on earth be welcomed with all your saints to the heavenly feast on the day of your kingdom; through Jesus Christ our Lord. Amen. *(BCP, Church of Ireland)*

*BLESSING

*DISMISSAL

Celebrant: Let us go forth in the name of Christ.
***People*:**   **Thanks be to God.**

7) But lo! There breaks a yet more glorious day;
   The saints triumphant rise in bright array;
   The King of glory passes on his way.
   Alleluia, alleluia!

8) From earth's wide bounds, from ocean's farthest coast,
   Through gates of pearl streams in the countless host,
   Singing to Father, Son, and Holy Ghost,
   Alleluia, alleluia!

* Please stand as you are able.

WORSHIP LEADERS

Celebrant: The Rev. Dr. Paula E. Gilbert

Preacher: Dr. Stanley Hauerwas

Deacon: The Very Rev. Timothy E. Kimbrough

Crucifer: Timothy McLeod, Middler MDiv

Torchbearer/Lector: Nicholas Krause, Middler MDiv

Torchbearer/Intercessor: Michelle Wolfe, Senior MTS

Cantor/Gospelbearer: Molly McGee, Senior MDiv

Thurifer: David Wantland, Middler MDiv

Sacristans: Stephen Crawford, Senior MDiv, and Christa Levesque, Middler MDiv

---

This liturgy is offered to the glory of God and for the benefit of the Duke Divinity School Community, its members, friends, and alumni.